INTERIOR DESIGN FOR LIBRARIES

Drawing on Function & Appeal

CAROL R. BROWN

AMERICAN LIBRARY ASSOCIATION
Chicago and London
2002

Composition by ALA Editions in Franklin Gothic and Bookman using QuarkXPress 4.1 for the PC

Printed on 50-pound white offset, a pH-neutral stock, and bound in 10-point coated stock by McNaughton & Gunn

The paper used in this publication meets the minimum requirements of American National Standard for Information Sciences—Permanence of Paper for Printed Library Materials, ANSI Z39.48-1992. ∞

Library of Congress Cataloging-in-Publication Data

Brown, Carol R.
  Interior design for libraries : drawing on function and appeal / by Carol R. Brown.
      p.   cm.
  Includes bibliographical references and index.
  ISBN 0-8389-0829-2 (alk. paper)
  1. Library buildings—United States—Design and construction. 2. Library decoration. 3. Library fittings and supplies. I. Title.
  Z679.5 B76 2002
  727.8′0973–dc21   2002001325

Printed in the United States of America

06 05 04 03 02   5 4 3 2 1

CONTENTS

ACKNOWLEDGMENTS

I would like to thank all the individuals who contributed either directly or indirectly to the preparation of *Interior Design for Libraries*. Most of my work on this book occurred after I left full-time consulting and took a position at the Fort Bend County Libraries (FBCL), headquartered in Richmond, Texas. Special thanks, therefore, go to Jane Powell and Roman Bohachevsky (current and former county librarians, respectively), who supported both my consulting work and the writing of this book. Several other Fort Bend County Libraries staff members assisted in my research. Molly Krukewitt, coordinator of youth services, was my advisor in matters concerning library service for children and teens. Jill Sumpter and Danea Hall of the library's technology staff helped with topics involving computers. Linda Lupro, formerly a staff member of the FBCL, provided me with research assistance for several years. I especially want to express my appreciation to Joyce Claypool Kennerly, who served as my general advisor, local editor, and technical consultant throughout the preparation of this book. I wish to thank all my other friends at the Fort Bend County Libraries who patiently listened to me talk about "the book" for two years.

I would like to thank Dana Rooks, director of the University of Houston Libraries, who took the time to discuss academic libraries with me. Thanks also to Joanne Downing and Eric Brown, who assisted with proofreading the manuscript.

I am extremely grateful to David Malman, of Architectural Lighting Design, who generously allowed me to use his information on lighting. Many architects and interior designers (and their staff) assisted me by providing information and photographs. The members of two architectural firms in particular spent hours with me discussing projects and their approach to the interior design of libraries. In this regard I would like to thank Denelle Wrightson and Maureen Arndt of Phillips Swager Associates for sharing information and numerous photographs and drawings for this book. Special thanks also go to Lynn Barnhouse, Jack Poling, and Jeff Scherer of Meyer, Scherer, and Rockcastle for supporting my work by providing information and photographs. Thanks especially to Jack for reading the manuscript and making excellent suggestions for changes.

Other architects and interior designers who assisted with this book include Daria Pizzetta and Deborah Kirschner of Hardy

Holzman Pfeiffer Associates; John Focke and Beth Walker of Ray Bailey Architects; Chuck Witt and Tammy Durrum of Johnson Romanowitz Architects; Ken English of Hermes Architects; Kirksey; Lynn Metz and Nicky Vidaurre of F & S Partners; and Bev Moris of Simon, Martin-Vegue, Winkelstein, Moris.

I would like to thank all the photographers who graciously allowed me to include their copyrighted work without paying usage fees. Their names are included with the photographs that they contributed to this book.

Several furniture manufacturers and sales representatives also provided photographs of their products for this book. I would like to thank Jerry Blanchet and MJ Industries; John Lumley and APW-Wright Line; Jill Randolph and ASI Sign Systems; Anne Kik and the Worden Company; Aaron Moser and Thos. Moser Cabinetmakers; Penny Schmitz and Libra-Tech; and Ty Peterson and Fetzers' Inc.

The names and contact information for all of the aforementioned appear in appendix B.

INTRODUCTION

The subject of interior design is relevant to both planning new and expanded library buildings and to renovating existing library spaces. The responsibility for interior design on a project may lie with an architectural firm, an interior design firm, or with architects and designers working together. In many smaller building projects, responsibility for the design of a library interior falls to the library director or to members of a library board.

The information in this book is intended for library planners, for architects and designers who have not built libraries in the past or who need to update their knowledge of library interior design, and for architects who are interested in hearing about interior design from a librarian's perspective. The information on library design presented here will provide first-time library planners with some basic resources needed to complete their project successfully. Most librarians will find themselves responsible for a renovation or a new building project at some time in the course of their careers. The information here should be helpful in making interior design decisions for library spaces of all sizes.

Hopefully, the topics discussed in this book will prompt a dialogue between the design professionals and the library staff working together on a building project. Architects and interior designers should listen carefully to staff requirements regarding adjacencies, visual control, and library policies and procedures. In turn, library staff, board members, and organization officials should allow design professionals to carry out their work without constant interference. Design professionals who have planned libraries successfully in the past should not assume that a library built several years ago can be a model for a library built in the 21st century.

The information presented here is relevant to any kind of library—academic, public, school, and special. The commonalities of interior design for libraries are greater than the differences. The missions of different types of libraries result in different spatial relationships within each type of building, but interior design issues are the same. All types of libraries have service desks, computer workstations, seating for users, shelving or storage units for materials, and staff work areas. All successful libraries are designed to provide comfort, convenience, attractive surroundings, and safety in functional spaces.

I am a librarian, rather than an interior designer, but over the course of more than 20 years of library consulting work, I have gathered information on the interior planning of libraries through working with dozens of architects and designers on numerous library projects. My additional research for writing this book involved interviewing interior designers and architects who specialize in library projects and studying the relevant literature. The information provided here is based on my own experience and knowledge. I freely acknowledge that other individuals may have views entirely different from the ones given here that may also result in successful library interior design.

By way of background for anyone unfamiliar with the role of the various design professionals in a building project, architects usually have an academic degree in architecture and are licensed by examination in the states in which they work. The architect is hired and is under contract by the owner of the project to develop all of the drawings and written specifications that are needed to construct or renovate a building. The architect hires any consultants needed for the project, including structural, mechanical, and electrical engineers and, sometimes, acoustical and lighting consultants. The architect usually puts the construction contract out to bid. Often the architect's scope of work also includes overseeing the construction of the library.

The work of an interior designer often overlaps the work of the architect. An interior designer may have an academic degree in interior design, and some U.S. states require interior designers to be licensed. Interior designers usually work on the details of the layout of the library, select and price furnishings, and are involved in choosing finishes for all aspects of the building. In many successful projects, the interior designer is involved in all aspects of planning the building, from programming to the library's opening day.

In many projects, the roles of architect and interior designer are not so clear-cut. In some architectural firms, architects provide interior design services, as well as planning the building. Many architectural companies have their own interior designers on staff; these designers may have architectural degrees as well as a background in interior design. In other cases, the architect or the library owner will hire an outside interior design firm to provide these services.

On some projects, a library consultant may be part of the planning team. A library consultant is often a person with library management experience who serves as a liaison between the local planning team and the design professionals. Some consultants are architects or interior designers. Sometimes the consultant is hired by the architectural firm and sometimes by the library. The consultant may be involved with programming and layout and may provide review services throughout the project.

Throughout this book, the word "staff" refers to library staff. The term "local planning team" refers to the individuals representing the library owner during the planning process. The team may include library staff; city, county, or organizational officials; members of library or other boards; faculty members; and other individuals designated to work with design professionals (architects and interior designers) during the planning of new or renovated library spaces.

Basic Considerations in Library Interior Design

Interior designers work with many of the same fundamental elements of design used by painters, sculptors, and other visual artists. Academic training in interior design usually includes a course on the basic elements and principles of design. For the interior design of libraries, the principles of design are used to create library spaces that are both functional and aesthetically pleasing.

An experienced interior designer uses the fundamentals of design in a manner that seems intuitive. When selecting furnishings, the basic design elements of form, size, and scale enter into the decision-making process. "Form" refers to the basic shape of an object (or a space) generated by lines, planes, volumes, and points. Individual furniture items are chosen with appropriate size and scale so that they are correctly proportioned to the overall size of the space and to other objects within it. Scale is an important consideration in regard to who will use the selected furnishings. For example, in order to provide furniture of the appropriate scale for children, the tables and chairs in a youth area are smaller than similar furniture in an adult area. Other design elements and principles considered in interior design are balance, harmony, rhythm, and emphasis.

While successful library interior design results from the application of the same elements and principles used in the interior design of any type of building, library design is distinctive because of the unique mission of all libraries. Libraries are usually nonprofit institutions that exist for the benefit of a company, an educational organization, or the residents of a governmental jurisdiction. While a larger organization or government pays for library services, users of a library rarely pay directly for services. A library has a particular mission to support the organization of which it is a part: a public library provides services to local residents; a school or academic library supports the curriculum of an educational organization; and a special library supports the work of a company or institution. A library is, therefore, a service organization.

Libraries are similar to modern bookstores in many ways. Both libraries and bookstores have ranges of bookstacks, comfortable seating areas, and service desks. Libraries also have work areas that are similar in design to those of commercial offices. Increasing use of computers and distance education in libraries has resulted in the inclusion of academic classrooms and computer labs in libraries. Only libraries, however, are designed with a unique combination of bookstacks, banks of computer workstations, classrooms and training areas, and meeting spaces that are "free" to users.

Because libraries are service organizations, the successful design of a library of any type (school, public, academic, or special) is based on careful consideration of several factors that enhance the use of the library by its clientele and support the work of the staff. Two of the most important factors are those of relationships, or adjacencies, and the movement of people and materials through the library. Architects, interior designers, consultants, and other members of planning teams should consider these and other factors during the design process.

Relationships, or Adjacencies

The terms "relationships," or "adjacencies," refer to the space-planning process in interior design. Space planning involves determining how large spaces within a building (like rooms and designated areas) will be arranged and relate to each other within each larger area. Likewise, it involves determining how furnishings and equipment will be arranged and relate to each other within each room and area. In other words, determining the relationships in a building involves deciding what spaces and functions will be adjacent to other spaces and functions.

Carefully planned relationships within a library serve to ensure that a facility will function successfully for both the public and the staff. A logically arranged library will be convenient and comfortable for users, will enhance self-help and wayfinding, and will provide a productive environment for the staff.

The relationships within a particular library are determined by studying that library's philosophy of service, its use of materials and services, and its policies and procedures. For example, the procedures for signing up for use of a computer in a public library or for obtaining reserved materials in an academic library are relevant to determining the relationships between service points and other library functions. As public-use computers have increased in number in all types of libraries, library philosophies have generally dictated that staff assist users at computer workstations from a nearby service desk. Online catalogs, by contrast, are frequently located throughout the library in stack areas to allow easy access to the catalog.

In most libraries, a circulation desk is located close to the main entrance, so that users can return books and make inquiries upon entering the building and can check out materials on the way out of the building. An information or reference desk may also be located within view of the main entrance, so that users can ask for directions when they come into the library. Collections of current magazines and newspapers in public libraries, and tables and carrels in academic libraries, are frequently located adjacent to windows so that users have a view of the outside while they are reading and studying.

Some common adjacencies in a public library relate to children's areas. Young children should not have to walk through adult spaces to enter the children's area, to walk to the circulation desk, or to use a rest room. If the library's community meeting room is used for children's story times and activities, the meeting room should be located adjacent to the children's room. Within a children's space, school-age young people should not have to walk through the preschool area to get to their own materials and services.

In a public library, the relationship of the children's and adult areas is an interesting consideration. In one library system, the children's area in a branch library was directly adjacent to the adult area. Users and staff complained frequently about the noise from the children; however, adults and children moved easily from one space to the other. In another branch, the library was L-shaped, with the children's area in one leg of the "L" and the adult area in the other leg. Users could access the circulation desk from the children's area without passing any adult materials. The staff believed that this arrangement had an adverse effect on the use of adult materials: adults brought children to the library, checked out children's materials, and didn't bother to go a few extra steps to the adult collections.

Adjacencies within a library are also determined by the need for visual control, which involves security, and the need to observe users who may need help. In small and medium-sized public libraries with no security staff, the layout of stack and seating areas may be determined by the need for visual control. Stacks can be lined up in a direction that allows staff an easy view down the aisles. Low stacks and seating can be placed in front of tall stacks in relation to service desks in order to prevent higher bookstacks from obscuring a clear view of seating areas or computer workstations from the desk. In order to maximize a small staff, a computer-training room or study rooms may have some glass walls and open off the reference area to give the staff visual control of the area.

Noise control is another defining factor in regard to locating spaces in the library. At one time, libraries were considered to be quiet spaces, with noise confined, for example, to the meeting room. Now, many library users have new attitudes about what is an acceptable noise level in a library. Extensive use of computers in libraries has resulted in more conversation between staff and users and between several users collaborating at a single computer. In determining adjacencies, consideration should be given to locating noisy library functions next to each other: circulation desks, browsing areas where users select audiovisual materials, and, possibly, the entrance to the children's area.[1] Quiet areas, such as reading and study space and periodical areas, are located away from the noisy functions. Computer-free rooms, quiet reading rooms, and individual study rooms placed in adult areas offer spaces where users can read in a quiet environment.

Because it has fewer materials and services, the smaller a library building is, the easier it is to determine relationships within the space. In a large academic or public library, however, determining relationships may involve studying the locations of departments and collections on several floors. The design of such a building must include, for example, consideration of how users access the materials (open or closed stacks), what subject areas are generally used together, and what is most convenient for users.

In a multilevel library, the adjacencies within a single floor must be planned. These adjacencies may include the relationship of the information desk to reference book collections and closed stacks, the relationship of faculty and staff offices and carrels to designated subject specialties, the relationship of online catalogs to ranges of open stacks, and consideration of where to place information desks for visual control.

The relationships between public and staff areas are based on consideration of library procedures and policies. The adjacencies should support the work of the staff as they provide service to the library's users. Generally, staff work spaces are close to the public-service areas relevant to the work of a particular staff. For example, in most libraries, the circulation desk is usually adjacent to the circulation work space, so that staff may move easily from staff to public areas as additional assistance is needed at the desk. Likewise, reference work space is usually located close to the reference desk. For the convenience of the staff, technical-services work spaces in small libraries are located next to the receiving area. Often, the director of a small library prefers to have his or her office close to the circulation desk. In an academic library with subject specialists, faculty members or specialists responsible for particular collections may have an office near their designated subject areas.

Another important consideration in planning staff areas is sometimes ignored by architects. In small libraries (or any library, for that matter), staff rest rooms should not open directly off the staff break or lounge room. Pleasant eating experiences are not enhanced by the sounds and odors from a nearby rest room.

In a large multistory building, it is imperative that the freight elevator be easily accessible from the loading dock and receiving area. If the technical-services department is located on an upper floor, the freight elevator must open onto this floor. Ideally, the freight elevator will open directly into the technical-services area.

The relationships within particular staff areas should be planned carefully. In a technical-services area, for example, the furniture and shelving layout should reflect the workflow and the movement of new materials through receipt and check-in, to cataloging, and finally to processing. In a small library, it may be necessary to lay out the space carefully to distinguish between the location where new, unprocessed materials come into the technical-services area and the location where processed materials are housed when they are ready to go to the shelves.

Movement of People and Materials through the Library

In an effort to design an aesthetically pleasing building, consideration of the functional importance of how people and materials move through the library should not be forgotten. ("Circulation through the building" is the term frequently used for this aspect of a facility; however, in library lingo, "circulation" more often refers to the check-out of materials.)

When designing the interior of a library, members of the planning team should take an imaginary walk through all parts of the building. The tour may be as simple as "walking" through the final layout of the building on paper, or the tour may be a virtual walk through the building using a computer-generated model.

In a small public library, the movement of materials and people is accomplished by planning the adjacencies as discussed in the preceding section. Library users can usually move easily from the building entrance to the adult or to the children's area or from the entrance to the community meeting room.

In a large building, however, careful planning of the movement of people and materials involves considering vertical movement from floor to floor, as well as horizontal movement across a single story. In one disconcerting situation in a large public library, users standing on one side of the building could look across a large atrium to the other side of the same floor; however, no obvious path from their side to the other side of the floor was visible. Neither users nor staff should experience the inconvenience of having to walk down stairs, or take an elevator down, and then walk back up stairs, or take an elevator back up, to get to the other side of the same floor. Library users in any building should be able to follow directions to any function in the building by way of a straightforward, logical path.

A library's staff move collections of books, periodicals, and audio-visual items around a building on a daily basis; the layout of a library should facilitate such movement. Logical arrangement of the building should support moving materials from the loading dock or receiving area to the technical-services area or, in the case of donated books, to a storage area. Both the vertical and horizontal movement of processed materials from technical-services areas to stack areas should be made convenient by providing adequately sized doors, aisles, and elevators, and by providing direct routes from processing areas to stack areas. Likewise, the route for moving returned materials from staff check-in and sorting areas back to the stacks in public areas should be logical and convenient. Doors or passages from staff areas to public areas should always be designed to allow for the convenient passage of a loaded book truck manned by a single person. In all but the smallest libraries, loaded book trucks should be moved from the sorting area to the public area through a door that lies directly between work and public areas; trucks carrying materials ready to be returned to the shelves should not have to travel through the busy area behind the circulation desk.

Other Interior Design Considerations

In addition to achieving functionally effective adjacencies and circulation, successful library design should result in attractive and comfortable spaces. In the second edition of *Interior Design*, John Pile states, "In an ideal world, every space that we enter and use would be designed not only to serve its purpose well but also to offer a visual experience that would be appropriate, satisfying, and even memorable."[2] An effectively designed library should offer just such a visual experience. (See figures 1 and 2.)

Furnishings, materials, colors, and lighting are just a few of the design elements in a building that make it an inviting place in which to be. In public libraries, one of the catchphrases often used in recent years is "the library as destination." In other words, library staff want people to come to the library because it is a comfortable, attractive, and pleasant place to spend some time, like a modern shopping mall, a park, or a movie theater.

A comfortable library is one in which materials and services are arranged in a logical manner, signage and other wayfinding elements assist with self-help, and furnishings are appropriate for their intended use. For example, satisfactory wayfinding devices to help the user include a clear and consistent sign system, a logical room layout that enhances self-help, visual clues such as color-coding of signs and furnishings, and changes in the color of carpet that indicate varying library areas. Shelving should be arranged in a logical manner that will assist library users in finding desired materials.

In a comfortable library, computer workstations may be at standing height for quick checks of the catalog or at seated height for

FIGURE 1

Main Library renovation, Texas Tech University, Lubbock, Texas. Architects, F & S Partners and Parkhill, Smith & Cooper, Inc. Used by permission of the photographer. Photo credit: Robert Suddarth Photographer.

involved Internet or database searching. Ergonomic task chairs may be provided at computer workstations, while standard reading chairs may be provided in quiet study areas. Reading and study areas may include both seating at tables and seating at individual study carrels. In children's areas or school libraries, chairs with several seat heights are provided for young people of all ages.

Successful libraries are also safe places designed to accommodate people of various physical and mental abilities. In public libraries, a facility must accommodate people of all ages in a safe environment. Design of a safe library includes consideration of such obvious factors as accessibility, lighting, and signage for emergency situations. Consideration should also be given to matters of flammability and toxicity when selecting carpets and upholstery; to the stability of chairs and shelving; and, in a children's area, to sharp corners.

Maintenance is an important design issue in nonprofit organizations, where funding is not often available for replacing worn and dirty carpets and for reupholstering, refinishing, or replacing furnishings. Maintenance factors are especially important in public or academic libraries with heavy use. Many materials and furnishings that can be used successfully in libraries with limited use or in residential design are inappropriate for heavily used library buildings. As a rule, libraries should not be built with interior elements that cannot be cleaned easily, such as broad, exposed beams visible from upper floors. Many libraries cannot afford the special equipment or contract services that would be needed to clean and maintain hard-to-reach building elements.

One of the major lessons librarians have learned over the last few years is the need to design libraries with internal flexibility. Modular

FIGURE 2

Chatham-Effingham-Liberty Regional Library, Savannah, Georgia. Architects, Hardy Holzman Pfeiffer Associates. Used by permission of the photographer. Photo credit: Robert Batey Photography.

library design with few load-bearing walls is an essential element of a flexible library. Walled spaces in the library must be planned to allow for changes in the future. Acoustical concerns make it necessary, for example, for libraries to design some walls that isolate spaces and that can be easily removed as library functions change. A public library may be designed with a glass "box" near the reference area that is used primarily for computer training; however, in the future, when computer use becomes as commonplace as turning on the television, special training areas may no longer be needed and can be removed.

Libraries planned now must be able to accommodate the unknown technology of the future. Libraries must be designed with an infrastructure that will allow for adding and moving computers easily and for relocating or replacing bookstacks and seating areas. Because we don't know the interior layout of the library in the future, lighting patterns should not be tied to the initial furniture and shelving layout. Good lighting should be available to library users regardless of how the spaces are arranged in the future.

Libraries are usually designed to be used for many years. During the life span of a library building, the staff, philosophies, policies, collections, and services will inevitably change. The library must be flexible enough to accommodate these changes easily and inexpensively. Often, library staff, board members, and officials have to be reminded to set aside their personal likes and dislikes and to concentrate on planning a library that is designed for an unknown future.

Selecting a carpet that was used successfully in the local doctor's office or choosing a furniture design because it looks great in someone's new house is not an effective way to make decisions during the interior design process. The recommendations of professionals who can take a more objective view of the design—architects, interior designers, and consultants—should be carefully considered in making final interior design decisions.

NOTES

1. Another philosophy suggests that high-interest browsing materials should be located beyond bookstacks, so that users may find books in which they are interested while walking to the browsing area.

2. John F. Pile, *Interior Design*, 2nd ed. (New York: Harry N. Abrams, 1995), 35.

The Planning Phases of a Library Building Project

Library building projects grow out of the realization by staff and users that a library is inadequate and out-of-date. The library can no longer carry out its mission and fulfill its long-range goals in the existing building. The bookstacks are all full; more computers, reader seating, and perhaps more meeting and training spaces are needed; and the library looks old and shabby. The library may no longer be large enough because its parent educational institution or governmental jurisdiction has grown substantially since the library was built. In recent years, many building projects are the result of more general changes in libraries. The computerization of library operations and resources has rendered building space insufficient and power and data distribution difficult to accomplish in older buildings.

Assessment and Recommendations for Improvements

Effective building projects—new buildings, expansions, and renovations—begin with an assessment of the existing building and a determination of what is required in the new or renovated space. Assessments and recommendations for building projects may be undertaken by an outside consultant or by a local planning team that may include library staff, faculty members and officials, and board members. Public libraries may use processes discussed in several books about library assessment, such as *Determining Your Public Library's Future Size,* by Lee Brawner and Donald Beck.[1]

The task of assessing a current library leads to the identification of what is generally needed in a new building. In order to determine the overall size of the new space, it is necessary to make decisions early in the planning process about the size and requirements of each individual functional space in the new building. The planning team will have to answer dozens of questions like the following:

> How many items should be housed in the new space? In other words, what should be the capacity of the building for books, audiovisual items, magazines, and other types of materials? What is the expected rate of acquisition and deacquisition (weeding) of materials?

How many seats for library users should be provided at tables and carrels and in lounge chairs? What is the maximum number of computer workstations required at locations throughout the building?

What special spaces, such as local history and genealogy collections, are needed?

How many and what types of meeting and training spaces are needed?

How many service desks will be needed?

What types and how many faculty and graduate student carrels and offices will be needed?

A local planning team, a consultant, or an architect uses the answers to these and many similar questions to determine the overall amount of space needed. Architects and consultants who have worked on libraries previously can apply square-foot values to a library's specific functions based on their past experience with library space planning or by applying standard formulas for library space to those functions. Square-foot formulas for many spaces and furnishings can be obtained from *Building Blocks for Library Space: Functional Guidelines*.[2]

Programming and Funding

Based on the assessment and recommended requirements, preliminary programming of a new building is completed in order to establish the amount of funding needed for the project. A library building consultant sometimes develops a preliminary program. After a budget is developed, funding is acquired. (Obtaining funding is often the most difficult and time-consuming part of a project.)

The overall project budget will include the cost of construction and all interior elements, such as carpet and other floor coverings, lighting, and millwork. The budget will also include an amount for furniture and shelving. Furniture and shelving budgets are often based on a per-square-foot allotment. In developing a budget for furniture and shelving, the following items should be considered:

The expected level of quality of the furniture.

The aesthetic requirements of the project.

The amount of standard furniture that will be used, as compared to custom-designed and -built furnishings that will require additional engineering or testing.

The expected quality and cost of materials and finishes to be used.

The amount of built-in electrical systems and accessories that will be specified with the furnishings.

The items that are to be included in the furnishings budget. (For example, service desks may be included in the construction budget as millwork items or may be included in the furnishings budget.)

Any existing furniture items that will be reused in the new or renovated building and any costs associated with refinishing these items.

Any expected increase in the cost of furnishings from the time the budget is established to the time the items are purchased.

After funding is obtained, a site has been acquired, and an architectural team selected, preliminary programming is refined and expanded by the architect working with an interior designer. The architect and designer review the initial assumptions of preliminary programming and provide the client with options for planning a functional library.

The final building program states the building requirements and serves as a guide during the design process for local planning team members, architects, interior designers, and other design professionals. As a project progresses through schematic design and design development, the planning team can check the plans, as drawn, against the information outlined in the building program, to ensure that the architect has carried out the requirements of the program.

Successful programming of both the architectural and interior design elements of a library begins with extensive dialogue between the design professionals and the library staff. The architect, interior designer, or library consultant programming a new or renovated building must spend time on-site in the existing building, meeting with staff and local planners in groups or individually. For small projects, an architect or a consultant preparing a building program may collect information during one site visit that lasts a day or two. For very large projects, a design team or library consultant may make several trips to the site and spend days, or even weeks, conducting community focus groups and meeting with local staff and planners before preparing a building program.

On small projects where a design team may have little experience building libraries, the architect and interior planners must meet with library staff and the local planning team to find out how the library operates and how the building can best serve the needs of expected library users. The architect or consultant programming a new or renovated building must obtain answers to the following types of questions. (Many of these questions are similar to those asked earlier when the overall amount of space for a new library was determined; however, more detailed information is needed at this phase of the project.)

Who uses the library; e.g., students and faculty of an academic institution, community residents of all ages, elementary and high school students and teachers, engineers working in the parent company, art students at nearby universities, etc.?

How is the library used; e.g., for quiet study as well as computer searching, to research case law, for children's activities, to complete homework and study for exams, to prepare for teaching classes, etc.?

How many staff members will work in the completed library? Where in the building will they work? How will they complete their work? Will they work "on the floor" but also have a workstation somewhere else in the building? What size of work area does each staff member need? How should work areas relate to public areas? What support-service areas are needed (technical services, public information, automation services, etc.)?

How does the library operate on a day-to-day basis?

What public services will be offered by the library; e.g., reference, circulation, programming for adults and children, computer and bibliographic instruction, interlibrary loan, mobile out-reach services, assigned study space, distance education, etc.?

What size are the collections to be housed in the library initially? What types of materials will be included in the collections?

How many computers will the building hold initially? Where will the computers be located in relation to collections and service desks?

What special areas will be required in the library; e.g., local history and genealogy room, media production areas, auditorium, green rooms for theatrical productions, Friends areas, etc.?

It is important for staff to provide very specific answers to these questions. Library staff may need to ask for guidance from the interior designer regarding the format of some answers. For example, if the staff supply information about collection size, the counting method—or formula for determining quantities—should be agreed upon by the library staff and the interior designer. The interior designer or consultant should be able to verify the quantities using the same counting method.

In building projects for large libraries, architects or consultants must also carry out information gathering in order to program a facility that meets the needs of a particular group of users and staff. A design team with extensive library-planning experience should not assume that information collected for similar library projects can be applied directly to other libraries that they design in the future. Experienced library architects can, however, facilitate the programming process by knowing what questions to ask and by offering library staff and the local planning team options in regard to building requirements that have worked successfully in other libraries.

Based on information collected by the design team, the details of the expected interior design of a new library are delineated in the *building program*. The building program notes the relationships or adjacencies required between various functional areas of the building, as well as relationships needed within a single department. The program lists the allocations of space and general requirements within the building and describes in detail the use, occupancy, and furnishings of each individual space. General requirements may include, for example, accessibility; heating, ventilation, and air-conditioning; lighting; and acoustics. Specific kinds of furnishings and other interior features are described in a separate building program section for each space.

The following is an example of a segment of a building program that describes an adult reference center in a public library.

Subarea	Square Feet
Adult reference desk	400
Reference book collection, 8,000 volumes, @ 108 vols. per double-faced section[3]	1,780
Computer workstations, 24 computers with printers, @ 60 square feet	1,440
Computer lab for training, 12 computer workstations, @ 60 s.f.	720
Small group/quiet/tutoring rooms, each with seating for four, 8 rooms, @ 150 s.f.	1,200
Study/tutoring rooms, each with seating for two, 4 rooms, @ 75 s.f.	300
Conference room	300
File cabinets, 8, @ 20 s.f.	160
Atlas case	40
Dictionary stand	25
Reader seats at tables for four, 32 seats @ 30 s.f.	960
Public copy room/alcove with counter, paper storage, and work area	200
Total size	7,525

Occupancy

Seating for 36 at computers; 32 at reader seats at tables and carrels; 40 at tables in small rooms; maximum of 3 staff members at one time

Adjacencies

The reference desk should be adjacent to the reference book collection, the computer workstations, and the computer lab. If possible, the small study rooms and the young adult area should be visible from the reference desk. The reference work area should be adjacent to, or close to, the reference desk.

Requirements

The reference center will include most of the adult services that require assistance for use. A reference desk located in the center of the area will be large enough to accommodate three people working there at one time. The reference desk should be visible from the entrance to the reference area. At least one 36"-wide section of the desk will be between 30" and 32" high, for wheelchair access required by the 1990 Americans with Disabilities Act (ADA). Privacy issues should be considered when designing the desk. One end of the desk, for example, may be designed as a special workstation for private discussions between a staff member and a library user. Ready-reference shelves and a work counter may be located behind the reference desk.

The reference book collection should be located on double-faced sections of shelving, preferably no more than 48" high, next to the reference desk. Equipment tables to hold 24 computers with printers for the catalog and reference sources in online and CD-ROM formats should be located close to the reference desk. The tables will be seated height; some will accommodate wheelchair access. Reader tables and carrels in the reference center should be equipped with tabletop access to power and to the library network.

A computer lab will be located in a separate walled room adjacent to the reference area. The lab will have glass walls above 42". When the room is in use for a training session, the door will be closed. When private training or classes are not being presented, the door to the lab will be open and the computers will be available as additional workstations for public use. The lab will also contain a covered white markerboard; an electrically operated, ceiling-mounted projection screen; and a mobile equipment cart or desk.

Small group or quiet study rooms will be located within view of the reference area. The rooms should have glass walls to allow for visual control from the reference desk and should be soundproofed. Each room will hold a table and two to four chairs. The rooms should be wired to allow for the use of laptop computers. The conference room should be supplied with a covered white markerboard and should have a counter and small sink behind closed doors to allow for coffee-making in the room.

A circulation desk and work area might be described in a building program as follows.

Adjacencies

A book-theft detection system will be located at the entrance/exit to the main part of the library. Requirements for the theft-detection system should be discussed with the appropriate vendor.

The circulation area should be close to the browsing area where high-interest items are stocked. The self-check station should be close to the circulation desk and visible from it, but should not be a part of the desk.

The circulation desk must be located adjacent to the foyer and visible from the library entrance. The desk must be directly adjacent to and open into the circulation workroom. The office for the circulation manager will be located inside the workroom. The desks for circulation staff and shared space for part-time staff should be in the area nearest to the door to the circulation desk.

Preferably, the check-in station (a computer workstation), sorting area, book truck storage, and the two book-drop areas will be adjacent to each other. The book return from the foyer should drop directly into the work area close to the check-in station. The drive-up book-return room should be in the same general area. Also, when planning the location of a drive-up pick-up window, consider that the pick-up window should not block access to the drive-up book return (and vice versa).

Requirements

Twenty to 25 feet of clear space should be left in front of the circulation desk to allow room for queuing. The location and shape of the desk should be planned to expedite the movement of library users waiting to conduct business at the circulation desk. The staff may prefer a desk with a zigzag design that indicates where patrons line up. Regardless of the design of the desk, the important matter of how people will line up in front of the desk should be considered and discussed with the Library Director.

Because staff will spend several hours at a time standing and working at the desk, the floor behind the desk should be cushioned in some manner. Eight to 10 feet of space should remain empty behind the circulation desk to allow for the movement of staff and book trucks. Consider designing the desk with special "docking areas" for book trucks and delivery bins. A door directly behind the circulation desk should lead to the circulation workroom. The door should not, however, provide a view into the workroom; people waiting at the circulation desk should not be able to look into the workroom. Offset doors or a short hall should lead from the circulation desk to the workroom.

The circulation desk may be constructed by a library-furniture manufacturer and may not, therefore, be part of the construction contract. The desk will, however, be planned in consultation with the architect at the same time the building is designed. The circulation desk will include a multicircuit electrical system that must be hardwired to the building power at one point.

The circulation desk must be large enough to accommodate a maximum of six people working there at one time. Staff will be checking out materials, registering users, and handling returned materials and fines. A workstation that matches the desk may be located on the wall behind the desk.

Several sections of shelving will be needed in the circulation desk area, or in the workroom in a space close to the desk, to hold reserved books waiting to be picked up by users. The section of the desk closest to the library entrance will include a book-return slot. The desk will have a level top (no transaction counter) at standard 39" standing desk height. A minimum of one 36"-wide section of the desk must be wheelchair height (30" to 32" high recommended) to comply with the ADA. This lowered area may be used as a card registration or children's check-out area, as well as providing a wheelchair-accessible station. A stool or chair that can be easily moved will be located next to the lowered area for patrons wishing to sit down while registering. (Alternatively, the staff may prefer a separate registration counter away from the circulation desk.)

The office for the circulation manager will be located in the work area. The office will contain a desk to accommodate a personal computer, a credenza with overhead storage, several bookcases, and a guest chair. The architect should discuss with the planning team the possibility of having some glass in the wall between the workroom and the circulation desk area, and glass in one wall of the office.

The circulation work area will include desks or workstations for full- and part-time staff. If space is available, the workroom will also include a built-in counter, approximately 15' long. The counter should be 29" high and should contain three knee spaces and have three pedestals with drawers below the worksurface. The counter should be 30" deep to accommodate computers. Built-in adjustable shelves should be built above the work counter. (This millwork will be part of the construction contract.) Access to power and data for the counter should be above the worksurface.

One section of the workroom will be the book-sorting area. The area will include sections of steel shelving, 90" high, for sorting returned materials prior to placing them on book trucks to be reshelved. A large open area for parking book trucks should be located next to the sorting shelves. The sorting area should include an area for storing bins containing books to be delivered to branch libraries.

A small room opening off the circulation workroom will provide access to the exterior drive-up drop for the 24-hour return of materials. The book-return chute should be located in such a manner that it can be accessed from the driver's side of an automobile; ADA standards apply, also. The location and placement of the book-return room (room that items drop into from the drive-up book return) should be discussed with the staff. Book-drop rooms are frequently a target for vandalism. The room must be an enclosed space equipped with a floor drain; two-hour, fire-rated walls; a smoke/heat alarm system; and an automatic fire extinguishing system. A second book/audiovisual-return slot in the foyer of the building will be used to drop returned materials into a depressible book truck in the workroom. Both of these book-return slots should be adjacent to the check-in computer workstation.

A future drive-up pick-up window will be staffed at specific times each week to allow users to drive by to pick up requested items without coming into the library. The pick-up area should have a secure, lockable window that can be unlocked when service is available. At least two sections of double-faced shelving should be located directly behind the window to house items to be picked up by users.

The following is an example of how a technical-services room might be described in a building program.

Requirements

The technical-services area is a nonpublic space where library materials are acquired and prepared for use. Technical-services functions include acquisitions, receiving, cataloging, and processing of all types of library materials.

A receiving area should be located next to the door through which deliveries and shipments of materials will be received. A small open space should be left in the receiving area for the temporary storage of materials and equipment coming into the building. The receiving area should include a table or counter for sorting mail, unpacking boxes, and preparing items for shipping. The receiving area will also need a computer for checking order records and storage space for postage meter, scales, and shipping supplies. Approximately 60 staff mailboxes should be located in the receiving area.

Computers will be used at work spaces throughout the area. A walled office for the head of technical services should be located adjacent to the work area for this staff. The office should have some glass walls to allow for a view into the adjacent work area. The office will contain a desk to accommodate a personal computer, a credenza with overhead storage, several bookcases, lateral files, and a guest chair. The work area will be furnished with approximately seven desks or workstations. The use of office panel-system dividers in the work area should be discussed with the planning team. A copier and a fax machine will be located in the work area.

Because book trucks will be moved frequently around the room, aisles between workstations should be a minimum of 48". The room will also contain the equivalent of 10–12 double-faced sections of 90"-high shelving and one or two worktables.

The power and data distribution system in this area should be as flexible as possible to allow for reconfiguring the space as the library changes. The interior of the space should be planned to reflect the flow of materials: purchase of materials, receipt and check-in of new items, cataloging, processing, and movement of materials out to the public area of the library. The interior layout and workflow should be planned in consultation with the library staff. The room should be planned so that there is a clear spatial distinction between those materials *coming in* for processing and those materials *going out* of the department to the public shelves and other work areas.

Each area of the technical-services department should be planned to serve the particular needs of the tasks performed there. The processing area, for example, will require extensive storage space for supplies. Millwork to hold boxes of book covers, laminating film, and other processing supplies should be planned in consultation with the staff.

A large walk-in storage closet will be located adjacent to the technical-services area. The closet should be furnished with 24"-deep industrial steel shelving to hold office and processing supplies.

Discuss the possibility of adding a staff conference room that will be available for staff meetings of the circulation and technical-services staff.

After a draft of the building program is prepared, the document will be reviewed by the local planning team and the architect. Changes and additions will be made to the program based on the review.

Schematic Design

With the building program complete, the architect begins the process of schematic design of the building. Deviations from the building program may occur during schematic design (and, occasionally, during design development) as the planning team and the architect agree that changes from the detailed requirements of the program may enhance the design of the building. It is essential that the interior designer work with the architect from the very beginning of the project. An architect cannot plan a successful building without considering the interior design of the spaces.

Sometimes, library staff who have planned for years for a new building try to draw the library on paper or in their thoughts prior to meeting the architect. The planning process will work more smoothly if the local planning team members do not have specific preconceived ideas about how the library should look or how it should be arranged. The architect is a professional who is being paid to do the design work.

Throughout the design process, it is the responsibility of the local planning team (library staff, board members, officials, facilities management staff) to carefully review all drawings to ensure that the plans are carrying out the intent of the building program. Members of the planning team should ask as many questions as necessary in order to understand the design of the library and how it works. Many architects prepare dimensional sketches or study models in order to help the local planning team understand the library design. (The planning team may request sketches or models if they have not been prepared by the architect and are needed to completely understand the design.)

When members of the local planning team believe that areas within the library (as drawn) will not function effectively, it is their job to point out their concerns to the architects. Members of the planning team may make suggestions for improvements; however, it is always the responsibility of the architect to find a solution to problems. It is sometimes necessary to make compromises during the design process, but functional considerations should prevail over aesthetic considerations.

The interior design of a library begins with a study of the relationships of the various functional spaces within the building. At the beginning of the schematic-design phase of a project, the architect or the interior designer will present the owner with diagrams that illustrate the relationships identified in a building program. The easiest drawings for a library planning team to understand are simple bubble diagrams that show the relationships within the building and, perhaps, the relative sizes of individual areas. Through a series of discussions between the architect, the interior designer, and the local planning team, the bubble diagrams will be refined and take shape as the earliest schematic drawings of the building interior. Members of the planning team should feel free to ask questions and make comments about both the diagrams and the early schematic drawings.

The schematic design may change several times before all parties agree that the relationships, as drawn, will work. Sometimes changes may be made later in the process as furniture and shelving are added to the plan. Schematic-design drawings will show the walls of rooms and door locations within the building. Early interior elevations drawn during the schematic-design phase will illustrate the preliminary locations and heights of windows and building entrances. Using the initial plans, the architects, interior designer, or building consultant will begin to draw preliminary furniture and shelving layouts in order to compare the capacity of the building, as drawn, with the building program requirements.

Design Development

The next phase of the building process is the design-development stage. During this phase, the architect begins refining the schematic plans. Mechanical, structural, and electrical engineers hired by the architect begin developing the details of the building. During design development, the interior designer, architect, or consultant refines the furniture and shelving layouts and begins making initial furniture selections.

During the design-development or construction-drawing phase, the interior designer will obtain budget prices for the initial furniture and shelving selections to ensure that the cost of furnishings will not exceed the allotted funds in the overall project budget. If the cost of initial furnishings chosen exceeds the funding available, changes must be made during later stages of the project; less expensive furnishings or fewer items must be substituted for initial selections and quantities in order to stay within the furnishings budget.

A budget for furnishings is usually based on information supplied by vendors. The interior designer, consultant, or a staff member prepares lists of furnishings desired and writes preliminary requirements or specifications for the items. The list is sent to a furniture vendor, or to several vendors, who will provide budget prices. If they know they have a good chance of being awarded the job, most vendors will supply budget pricing. In situations where state or local regulations and a local purchasing department do not want the library to work solely with one vendor, the list of possible furnishings can be sent to several vendors and those vendors who are interested will each supply budget prices. In projects that involve bidding, budget prices received from vendors will be higher than the vendor's final bid price; vendors do not want to show their hand completely in the early stages of a project.

Development of Construction Drawings

The last planning phase of a building project is the one during which the architects prepare the construction (or working) drawings and detailed specifications that will be used in constructing the building. A construction contractor is awarded the job based on bidding from the construction drawings and specifications. (Most projects involve two bidding processes, one for building construction and one for furnishings.)

During this phase, interior planning involves working with the architect and interior designer to plan the specific details (dimensions and materials) of any built-in furnishings such as counters, cabinets, and bookcases. All of the interior finishes will be selected, such as plastic laminates for built-in counters and cabinets, carpets and other flooring materials, paint or vinyl wall coverings, rest-room tile, etc.

For a small project in which the construction will be completed in a year or less, final furniture and shelving selections should be made during the period of time that the construction drawings are being prepared. For a large project that will take more than a year for building construction, final furniture selections may be made during the time that construction of the building occurs. Additional budget pricing may be obtained after final furniture selections are made, to determine that the furniture choices remain within the allotted budget.

After final furniture and shelving selections are made, the interior designer works with the project team to choose colors, finishes, and materials for furnishings. Furniture and shelving selections are documented in specifications prepared by an interior designer, consultant, or architect. In public projects that require a bid process for furniture, the specifications become the major part of the furniture bid document. In a small project, the selection of finishes and the preparation of specifications and bid document can be completed while construction drawings are prepared or in the first six months of building construction.

In large projects, such as the construction of a main library for a city, the entire furniture, shelving, and finish selection process and the preparation of bid documents may take a year or more. Prototypes or mock-ups of custom-designed furnishings may be built. The design team may visit furniture factories to determine which companies have the human resources and facilities to complete the project within the desired time period.

After a bid document is prepared for furnishings, the project is put out for bid by the institution or organization that is the "owner" of the project. (Alternatively, when bidding is not required, prices are negotiated with vendors.) The period of time needed for bidders to complete their bid varies according to the complexity of the project. In a small project with mostly standard or customized versions of standard furnishings, bidders can be expected to return their bids in four weeks. In a large, complex project that requires the making and submission of samples, the bid period may stretch into months.

After bids are received, the period of time required to award bids also varies with the size of the project. A small project with bids that can be easily evaluated and awarded quickly by a local council or board may have bids awarded within three weeks or a month. A complex project, however, may take a month or more to evaluate. In situations where the governing body does not agree with the recommendations made by the planning team or the design professionals, the process of awarding bids may be prolonged while additional bids are sought or time is spent justifying the recommended awards to officials.

After bids are awarded, vendors are required to prepare shop drawings for some of the furnishings specified. Shop drawings illustrate in detail how custom items, and sometimes standard items, will be constructed. Vendors are required to submit shop drawings to the owner for approval. The drawings will be reviewed by the interior designer, the architect, or a consultant. Many shop drawings require some redrawing to correct misinterpretation of the written specifications. On a project of any size, when the shop drawings must be reviewed and redrawn several times, the shop drawing approval stage of the project may take two or three months. On a large project, of course, the time may be longer.

Library furnishings are placed in a production queue by a factory, once shop drawings have been approved. Furnishings for small projects (buildings less than 100,000 square feet) can be produced by a number of factories. Furnishings for large projects, like the 375,000-square-foot San Francisco Main Library, can only be produced by factories with the capability for extensive projects.

When an order for furnishings is placed in a factory's production schedule, the vendor will notify the interior designer or consultant of the projected shipping date for the completed furnishings. This date, as well as the expected completion date of the building construction, may change several times during the course of the project. The interior designer and vendor will communicate several times to adjust either the building completion date or the expected delivery date of the furnishings.

The production time needed for furnishings or shelving depends on the quantities of furniture required, the complexity of the design of custom pieces, the availability of materials, and the total workload of the factory. The lead time for receiving furniture can also vary according to the time of year the order is placed.

In summary, the time required for furniture production depends on the size of the project, the circumstances of the manufacturer, and other unknown factors. In order to determine a tentative schedule to cover the time frame from bidding through delivery, interior designers or consultants must discuss the expected schedule with possible bidders. To set an initial schedule, it may be easier to begin with the expected delivery date following building completion and work backward.

Often, library staff or other local officials will set the date of the grand opening of a new library without consulting the interior designer about reasonable delivery dates of furniture. The disappointing result can be that the library is opened with some furniture not yet on-site. The interior designer or consultant understands furniture production and works closely with a vendor or manufacturer to estimate the delivery and installation date of furnishings. In order to ensure that the building interior will be complete before the grand opening, the date of the event should not be determined too far ahead of building completion, and the opening date should be set in consultation with the interior designer and the architect.

The following is an example of an ample time schedule for the purchasing of furnishings for a 30,000-square-foot building. The schedule would obviously take much longer for a larger building.

Bid documents prepared	April–June 2003
Items go out for bid	July 1, 2003
Bids due	July 31, 2003
Bids evaluated	August 1–31, 2003
Bids awarded	September 30, 2003
Shop drawing phase	October 1–December 31, 2003
Production of furnishings	January 1–June 30, 2004
Expected completion date of building	June 30, 2004
Delivery of all furnishings	July 1–31, 2004

NOTES

1. Lee B. Brawner and Donald K. Beck Jr., *Determining Your Public Library's Future Size: A Needs Assessment and Planning Model* (Chicago: American Library Association, 1996).

2. *Building Blocks for Library Space: Functional Guidelines* (Chicago: American Library Association, 1995).

3. Twenty-four square feet per double-faced section.

3 Basic Interior Design Issues

During the schematic and design-development phases of a project, building planning requires the integration of decisions regarding library architecture, engineering, and interior design. The process of planning the interior of a library begins with the architectural design of the building, but because architectural structure determines the basic sizes and shapes of interior spaces, consideration of the library's interior design must occur simultaneously with designing the exterior of the building. (See plates 1A and 1B.)

A functional library cannot be designed by planning how the building will look on the outside until the relationships, relative sizes, and necessary shapes of areas needed in the interior have been studied. A library design that begins, for example, with planning an attractive exterior intended to please the city council but with little or no regard for interior function may not be a successful library building.

Library Shape

In determining the basic shape of a new library, library architects and consultants agree that the most functional shape for a library is a square, or a series of squares. Architects sometimes see this shape as too simple and uninteresting; however, long, narrow spaces and round rooms do not allow for the efficient layout of ranges of shelving or for good visual control by staff. Nor do narrow or round spaces provide the flexibility of squares. Aaron and Elaine Cohen express the desirability of the square in library buildings as follows:

> With a square, there is more floor area in relation to the confining envelope than other easy-to-build configurations. A square is also simple to divide and rearrange. Cut in two and the result is two small rectangles. Cut in four and the result is four small squares. No matter if the library is large or small, to be built from the ground up or simply rearranged, the square always works.[1]

Modular Design

Successful libraries are designed with few load-bearing walls and with large, flexible spaces that can be easily rearranged as library needs change. The engineering of the library structure should be done early in the planning process, either prior to or at the same time that initial shelving layouts are being planned. The basic bays or modules of the building structure (recurring dimensions between columns) should be planned to accommodate the efficient layout of ranges of shelving from column to column. It is disconcerting as a consultant or interior designer to lay out the shelving with the columns in one configuration, only to be told that the distance from column to column was only an approximation and that the locations of columns will be changing.[2]

The size of bays should allow for easy integration of bookstacks and furnishings into the library design. Bays should be designed to accommodate standard double-faced shelving units, 36" wide × 24" deep, with aisles a minimum of 36" wide (42" wide is preferred by the Americans with Disabilities Act). Some public or school libraries may prefer aisles 48" wide. If 36"-wide aisles are planned, it should be noted that the depth of a double-faced section of shelving is a *nominal* 24". Most bookstacks have an actual depth of more than 24" at the base, and when end panels are added, the actual depth of the bookstacks at the point of the end panel can be 2" to 3" more than the nominal depth of 24".

Ceiling Heights and Location of Windows

In addition to the size of bays in a building, it is often necessary to know ceiling heights in the major areas of the building and the locations and sizes of windows prior to laying out the building interior. The architect and interior designer must, therefore, work together on these issues from the very beginning of a project. For example, an architect may design a building with a low ceiling over stack areas and a higher ceiling over a center axis of the building. The architect and the interior designer should agree that the various ceiling heights will enhance the functionality of the space as a library and not adversely affect required relationships. In public and school libraries where wall shelving is used, the location and height of windows and soffits may be crucial factors in determining the location of stacks and, ultimately, the shelving capacity of the space. (See figure 3.)

Power and Data Locations

The use of computers throughout a library has confirmed the need to plan the structure and systems of the building simultaneously with the interior design. Because libraries and technology change continuously, buildings must be designed with built-in flexibility for providing and changing power and data locations wherever they are needed in the future. Even if data transmission becomes wireless in most buildings, the need for power at computer locations will continue.

Modular construction with columns helps to provide a means of ensuring that power and data are available to all parts of the library. Power and data lines can run inside a column from the ceiling to a few inches above the floor. When designing columns, architects might consider the need for columns to carry power and data lines. Solid wood or solid steel columns that are not furred out decrease the flexibility of the building for accommodating power and data.

Columns cannot be used, of course, for supplying power and data to open floor spaces. Plans for running power and data lines through a building are usually based on the size of the building and the project budget. Most small libraries with limited budgets run power and data through the building slab, using standard conduit terminated at specific locations in the floor. Architects and electrical engineers with limited knowledge of libraries may not understand the need for an extensive grid of conduit in reading table, carrel, computer, and reference areas. It is sometimes the responsibility of the library planning team to insist on building in power and data conduit in areas where computers will not be used initially. Also, it is necessary to provide power and data in areas that are initially built for bookstacks. In some libraries built 10 years ago or less, stack areas have already had to be reduced or reconfigured in order to accommodate more computers. It cannot be assumed that any area of the library initially used for bookstacks will always be used for them.

Library projects with larger budgets and spaces may be built with extensive under-floor duct systems (like Robertson duct) installed in a regular grid that provides flexibility in moving power and data locations. Standard ductwork may be used in some areas of the library, while an under-floor grid system is installed in areas that are expected to house the most computers—reference areas, reading areas, and technical-services workrooms. When furniture placement and electrical plans are developed at the same time, power and data can be provided from walls to carrels and tables.

In summary, regardless of how power and data are handled in the building, decisions about the interface of the building system and the use of furniture must be made together. The architect must provide a blueprint that overlays the building's power and data system over the furniture layout. The ultimate goal is to avoid having to use a power pole for power and data in the library at some time in the future.

Other Building Elements

Some interior building elements are controversial additions to public and academic libraries. The inclusion of an atrium in a library, for example, should be considered carefully. Where effective use of resources is a particular concern to an organization or community, an atrium that is aesthetically pleasing but occupies a large amount of interior space may be a public relations disaster. The library's public may see the atrium as wasted space that could have been used for bookstacks, computers, and seating. Moreover, an atrium entails nonfunctional space that must be heated, ventilated, and air-conditioned.

Other interior elements that should be considered carefully are interior fountains (often a maintenance headache), gardens (water for the plants can have an adverse impact on the environment for books), and any body of water that has the potential for causing accidents or attracting children. In children's areas, structures that encourage climbing, jumping, or running should be avoided. As plans for a library proceed, it is important to consider the locations of small building items in relation to larger furnishings. It is disconcerting, for example, to find late in the planning process that a fire extinguisher is on a wall where shelving is to be installed.

Planning the Furniture Arrangement

Planning the furniture placement in a library involves trying out various arrangements. The design professional working on the interior layout draws various schemes for main public areas before deciding on the best options to show to the planning team. The local planning team reviews the presented drawings, suggests changes, or asks for additional drawings. The use of computer-assisted design (CAD) programs in interior design allows the architect or designer to make changes easily and quickly.

Furniture and shelving layouts should reflect the adjacencies outlined in the library building program. If the drawings do not reflect the programmed relationships, the planning team should express its dissatisfaction and ask the design professionals to offer additional options. Members of a successful planning team should voice their concerns and may offer suggestions for changes.

Planning library furniture and shelving layouts involves considering universal design factors that ensure the library will be convenient and comfortable for people of all ages and abilities. The philosophy of universal design incorporates existing laws, such as the Americans with Disabilities Act, as well as the spirit of the law to ensure accessibility and comfort for everyone.

Furniture arrangement and the selection of individual pieces of furniture are tasks that involve consideration of human factors that affect how people react within an environment. One of the relevant human factors in library interior design is the concept of acceptable personal space; that is, how closely can people sit or stand next to each other and continue to feel comfortable? In the United States, in a social context like a library, most people are comfortable at a distance of four to five feet. In intimate conversations, however, individuals may be comfortable at a distance of less than four feet. Different cultures have different attitudes toward what is an acceptable space between people in various social situations. In many countries, a comfortable distance in a social setting can be less than four feet.

In addition to a desire for personal space, individuals have a need to define their "territory." For example, seating at a single carrel in a library clearly defines one person's territory. The desire for personal space and territory are demonstrated by the manner in which library users select seats at a reading table. Strangers prefer sitting across from each other, rather than side-by-side. People sitting side-by-side prefer to have some space between themselves and the person seated next to them. The first person to take a seat at a table for six, for example, usually takes a seat at one end of the table, and the second person takes a seat at the far end of the table on the other side. In a crowded library, two more people may take seats at the other two corners of the table; however, only in a very crowded library will anyone take the middle seat between the people on the ends. Sometimes when people are forced to sit close together, they will set up a psychological barrier between themselves and others (a pile of books) or will change their body language (turn their back toward the other person).

A similar concern for personal space occurs when users select lounge seating in a library. When lounge chairs are placed side-by-side, individuals often leave an empty seat between themselves and another person. Sofas can be used in children's areas where a young person and a caregiver sit together to read, but two- and three-seat lounges are not generally used in most library areas, because two strangers will not sit next to each other on a couch.[3]

In order to design a furniture layout, preliminary decisions must be made about the types of furniture to be used. Libraries should be planned with a variety of spaces and furnishings that will accommodate many different personal preferences. Rectangular tables, for example, are often used by people who are working alone. Round tables, however, suggest working together. Some people prefer to be at a table where they can look around and see what is going on in the area, while others like a semiprivate space—like a carrel with side panels—where they can look up and see others, but still have a sense of privacy. More small tables for four rather than larger tables for six are preferred because of people's attitudes toward personal space and territory—the middle seats at a table for six are often wasted space.

Academic libraries have individually assigned carrels or offices. In public libraries, small study rooms with seating for one to six are provided for quiet study, tutoring, and small group projects. Groups of teenagers like small study rooms or round tables where they can talk and study together. Young children like small, cubbyhole spaces, where they can crawl in to look at books alone. Children also need spaces where they can sit down with a caregiver to share a book.

In public and school libraries, the relationship between seating, stacks, and service desks is especially important. Ranges of tall bookstacks should not be placed directly in front of service desks; computers and seating should be between service desks and tall stacks in order to give the staff a clear view of users seated at tables and computers. In large libraries, stacks are often arranged around the perimeter of the room, while reference desks, seating, and computers are arranged in the center of the room.

When planning for a line of reading tables or carrels where the chairs of one table/carrel will be back-to-back to the chairs of the next table/carrel, the tables/carrels should be arranged with a minimum of five feet of space from one worksurface edge to the next worksurface edge. If space is available, an even larger aisle should be planned between tables or carrels. In public libraries, tables may be arranged in lines of six or seven or in small groups of four to six, while in academic libraries, dozens of tables may be arranged in study-hall style in a large room.

The arrangement of lounge seating depends on the expected use of the chairs. Single lounge seats for quiet reading are often separated by an open space of three feet or more, or by an occasional table. An area for quiet reading may have some lounge chairs placed back-to-back. Lounge chairs that are placed closer together and face-to-face suggest that the area is appropriate for conversation. Face-to-face lounge seating, for example, might be used in a children's area where caregivers converse while their children are in a nearby story time.

Computer tables are usually arranged within view of a service desk, so that assistance is nearby. The arrangement of computer areas depends on the type of tables that will be used for holding the equipment. Preliminary decisions about computer furniture have to be made during the later stages of the schematic-design phase of the project in order to coordinate the furniture layout with electrical plans. In reference areas, both academic and public libraries need banks of computers that are efficiently arranged on some kind of double-faced, starter/adder type of furniture supplied with an integrated electrical system. Users spend long periods of time at computers and want space around the computer to hold books and personal items. Each computer worksurface should be 48" to 60" wide and 36" deep, overall. When banks of computers are arranged with chairs backing from both sides into an aisle, the tables should be seven to eight feet apart to allow for the passage of a user or staff member between the chairs.

Academic libraries often have large computer areas (information arcades, for example) that are designed for both group and individual use of computers. Six-sided modules with two or three seats at each computer workstation have worked successfully in this situation.

Academic and public libraries may include computer-training labs. Libraries can make efficient use of computers and space by designing a computer lab close to a reference area. The lab is a separate room with glass walls that can be closed during a training session for staff or the public. When a class is not in session, the room can be left open, providing users access to additional computer workstations for individual work. (See plate 2A.)

Computer labs may be arranged in classroom style, with all participants facing the instructor, or they may be arranged with the workstations located around the perimeter of the room, with users

FIGURE 4
Main Library renovation, Texas Tech University, Lubbock, Texas. Architects, F & S Partners and Parkhill, Smith & Cooper, Inc. Used by permission of the photographer. Photo credit: Robert Suddarth Photographer.

facing the wall. In either arrangement, the instructor must be able to walk behind computer users to view their screens during a training session. Computer labs may also be designed to serve as teleconferencing and distance-education labs; therefore, seating arrangements must allow for a view to individual computers, to the instructor, and to videoconferencing equipment. (See figure 4.)

The usefulness of a computer lab can be increased by locating one or more small conference rooms adjacent to it. The rooms can be used for classroom training that does not involve hands-on access to computers and for breakout sessions that are part of a presentation.

Stack Areas

In public libraries, stack areas are often interspersed with reading areas to make the atmosphere more casual and less "academic." In college and university libraries, however, large stack areas are planned for the most efficient use of space for collections. In public and school libraries, ranges of bookstacks may be used to delineate particular areas in the library: adult and juvenile, preschool and school-age, middle school and high school. In any kind of library, stacks should be arranged to allow for shelving books in a logical sequence with either the Dewey Decimal or Library of Congress classifications. Users should be able to find a call number easily without the help of a staff member.

Standard sections of wood or steel shelving are 36" wide, though 24"- and 30"-wide sections are also available. Double-faced, free-standing shelving should be drawn 24" deep on initial furniture layouts. Single-faced wall shelving should be drawn 12" deep, although in final furniture selections later in the process, shelving may actually be 20" or 10" deep in some areas. Sections of shelving are installed together to form a range. In public libraries, a rule of thumb suggests that ranges of shelving should not be more than six sections, or 18 feet, long. In academic libraries, however, ranges are often longer than six sections.

At the corners of a room where two ranges of steel wall shelving meet, the two ranges should not overlap. Special square filler sections (10" × 10" or 12" × 12" × the height of the shelving) can be used to finish off the empty corner.

As previously noted in the discussion about the size of building modules, the aisles between bookstacks must be a minimum of 36" wide, with 42" aisles preferred by the ADA. Sometimes public and school libraries have aisles 44" or 48" wide.

It is a generally accepted practice that cross aisles between groups of ranges are a minimum of five feet wide. The minimum width of cross aisles or aisles at the end of a bookstack range is defined by the ADA as follows. Section 4.3.3, "Accessible Route, Width," in *ADA Accessibility Guidelines for Buildings and Facilities*, states: "The minimum clear width of an accessible route shall be 36 in. (915 mm) except at doors. . . . If a person in a wheelchair must make a turn around an obstruction [such as the end of a range of shelving], the minimum clear width of the accessible route shall be as shown in Fig. 7 (a) and (b)."[4] Figures 7A and 7B show that two 90-degree turns in a wheelchair around an object a minimum of 48" wide requires a 36" aisle; however, two 90-degree turns in a wheelchair around an object *less than 48" wide* requires a 48" aisle." In other words, a 24"-deep bookstack range requires an end aisle a minimum of 48" wide. Application of the ADA is, of course, a matter of interpretation, so some architects believe that a 36" aisle at the end of a range is acceptable. In some cases, the width of the aisle will be determined by a local or state ordinance and may be somewhere between 36" and 48". In order to ensure accessibility for everyone, 48" aisles are preferred at the end of ranges.

In small public libraries with limited staff, ranges of bookstacks are often arranged perpendicular to the service desk in order to allow staff to look down the aisles more easily, for security reasons, and to see users who may need assistance. In school libraries, bookstacks may be used to delineate separate seating areas for several classes.

Building Examples

Maribelle M. Davis Library, Plano, Texas; Architects, Phillips Swager Associates

The Davis Library is a 30,000-square-foot building that is part of a library system whose technical-services operations are located in another library. (See figure 5.) The public entrance to the library leads into an area that can be used when the main part of the library is closed. For before- or after-hours meetings, the public can access the meeting room, rest rooms, kitchen, and related storage without entering the library proper. Although the meeting room can be secured from the rest of the building, the meeting room is adjacent to the children's area of the library. Young people can pass directly from the children's area into the meeting room for puppet shows and other activities presented for large groups. Small groups of children can participate in programs in the story-time room in the children's department. Or the staff of the library can hold two presentations simultaneously by using both the story-time area in the children's department and the meeting room. (See plate 2B.)

In this library, the children's space is a separate room with a glass wall at the entrance that allows a view into the room from the adult area. The walled room allows children to be themselves without disturbing adults who prefer a quieter library environment. The children's reference desk is located adjacent to the main entrance, so that users can ask for assistance upon entering. Computers are located close to the librarian's desk, so that staff can provide help easily and maintain visual control of the use of the equipment. Preschool book collections and book collections for

DAVIS PUBLIC LIBRARY

PLANO, TEXAS

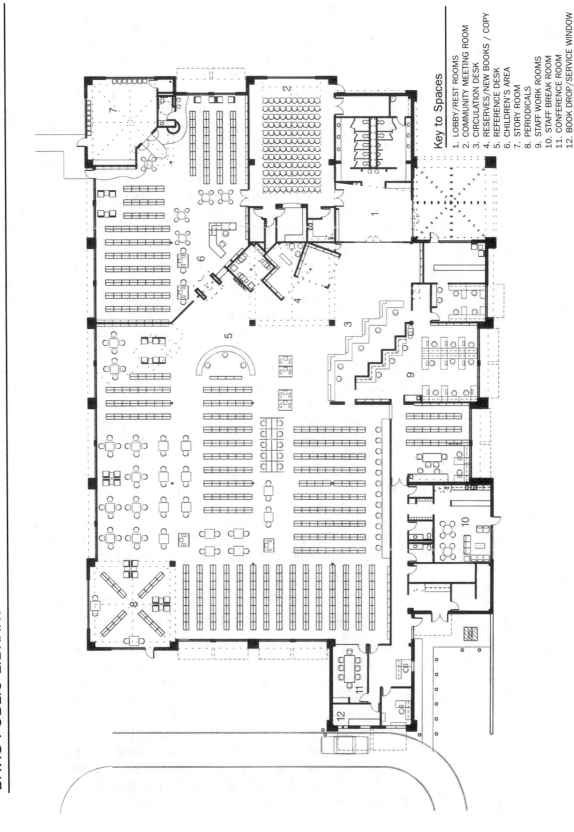

Key to Spaces

1. LOBBY/REST ROOMS
2. COMMUNITY MEETING ROOM
3. CIRCULATION DESK
4. RESERVES/NEW BOOKS / COPY
5. REFERENCE DESK
6. CHILDREN'S AREA
7. STORY ROOM
8. PERIODICALS
9. STAFF WORK ROOMS
10. STAFF BREAK ROOM
11. CONFERENCE ROOM
12. BOOK DROP/SERVICE WINDOW

FIGURE 5

Davis Library, Plano, Texas. Architects, Phillips Swager Associates. Used by permission of the architects.

school-age children are separate, so that older children do not have to pass through the "baby" area to get to their books. A family rest room is provided.

For the convenience of users, the library circulation desk is located right inside the main entrance. A book drop close to the library entrance allows users to drop off returned books as soon as they enter. The stairstep design of the circulation desk provides an indication to library users of how to line up for checking out books. Two self-check stations are located close to the circulation desk, so that staff can assist users the first time they use the self-check equipment. The workroom is located directly adjacent to the circulation desk so that additional staff may be summoned when more help is needed at the desk.

In this library, materials that have been reserved by users are not stored behind the circulation desk and retrieved by staff. Rather, the books are shelved in an alcove in the public area of the library and retrieved by the users themselves.

The young adult section of the library is located close to the children's area, but in the adult area. The young adult area is located within easy view of the reference desk, so that staff may easily maintain visual control. The audiovisual collections—popular materials in public libraries—are located next to the young adult area.

The adult reference desk is located in the center of the adult area and within view of the main entrance to the library. The reference book collection is located behind the desk for easy access by the staff. The reference stacks are 42" high, so that the staff have a better view across the room. Computer workstations are placed near the desk, so that staff can easily assist users. The periodicals are in a separate space that provides a view to the outside and is away from the noisy area around the reference desk. A conference room that can be used for staff and public meetings is located at the back of the adult area.

Other back-of-the-house areas include a drive-up, outside book drop, the branch manager's office and reception area, delivery entrance, and the staff lounge and rest rooms.

Sugar Land Branch, Fort Bend County Libraries, Sugar Land, Texas; Hermes Architects

This branch library is 20,000 square feet in size; technical-services operations are located in the system's main library. (See figure 6.) The main entrance to the library provides access to the meeting room, rest rooms, kitchenette in the meeting room, and related storage. A drop-down gate can be lowered to lock off the meeting room module from the rest of the library. Upon entering the library, the children's area is located in the right wing of the building and the adult area is located in the left wing. Drops for returned materials are provided outside the entrance to the building and in the foyer. Returned materials drop directly into the workroom.

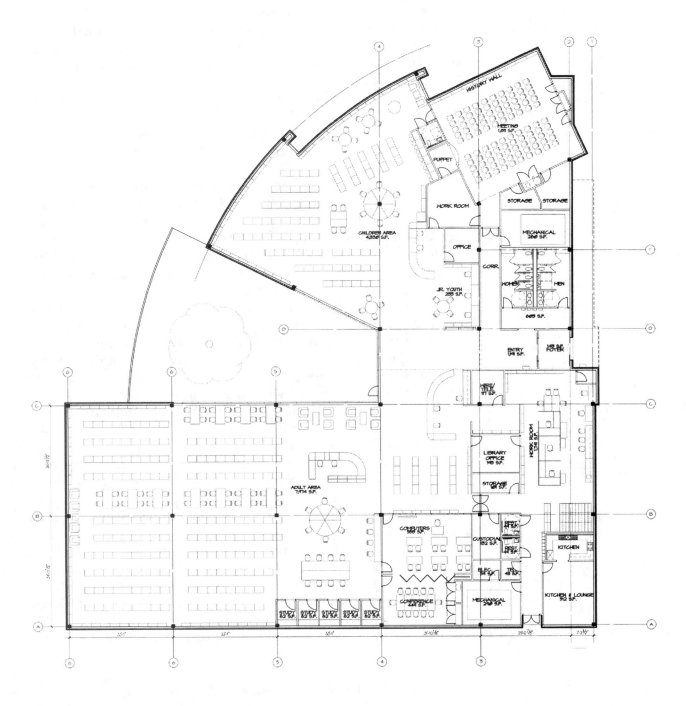

FIGURE 6

Sugar Land Branch, Fort Bend County Libraries, Sugar Land, Texas. Hermes Architects.
Used by permission of the architects.

The circulation desk is located directly to the left of someone entering the building. The corridor to the workroom, located behind the desk, includes bookstacks for shelving reserved books to be picked up by users. The workroom for all staff is located adjacent to the circulation desk.

The young adult area in this library (referred to as "jr. youth" in the plan) is a separate section of the children's area. It is located directly inside the entrance to the area so that young adults do not have to pass through the preschool and school-age areas to get to their space.

In this building, all children's group activities occur in the meeting room, which is directly accessible from a door in the children's area. A children's rest room is provided. The children's reference desk is located within easy view of the entrance to the area. Computers are located close to the reference desk. The children's librarian's office, the workroom, puppet theater, and meeting room are adjacent to the reference desk.

The library's audiovisual collection is located next to the circulation desk, in a highly visible space. The branch has the capacity for 30 adult computers. Twelve computers are located in the computer lab, which is located within easy view of the reference desk. When the computer lab is needed for classes for the public or staff, the door to the room is closed. When classes or demonstrations are not in progress, the room remains open and the computers are used by the public as additional workstations.

An electrically operated, movable partition separates the computer lab from the adjacent conference room. When additional seating is needed in the computer room, the partition can be folded back. The conference room can also be used for breakout sessions as part of computer training or as a general conference room for meetings by public and staff.

The adult area of the library includes five study rooms that can be used for quiet or group study. The reference desk is located at the entrance to the adult area. Periodicals are on the shelves next to the window seating. Reference books are located on the shelves closest to the reference desk. Adult fiction is housed on one side of the main aisle and adult nonfiction is housed on the other side of the aisle.

Hedberg Library, Carthage College, Kenosha, Wisconsin; Architects, Meyer, Scherer & Rockcastle, Ltd.

The Carthage College library is a 65,000-square-foot facility constructed in 2001. The library serves the faculty and the 2,250 part- and full-time students of the college. (See figures 7A and 7B.)

The layout of the Hedberg Library illustrates some of the differences between public and academic libraries. The building has two floors: a ground floor that is partly below grade and a first floor that

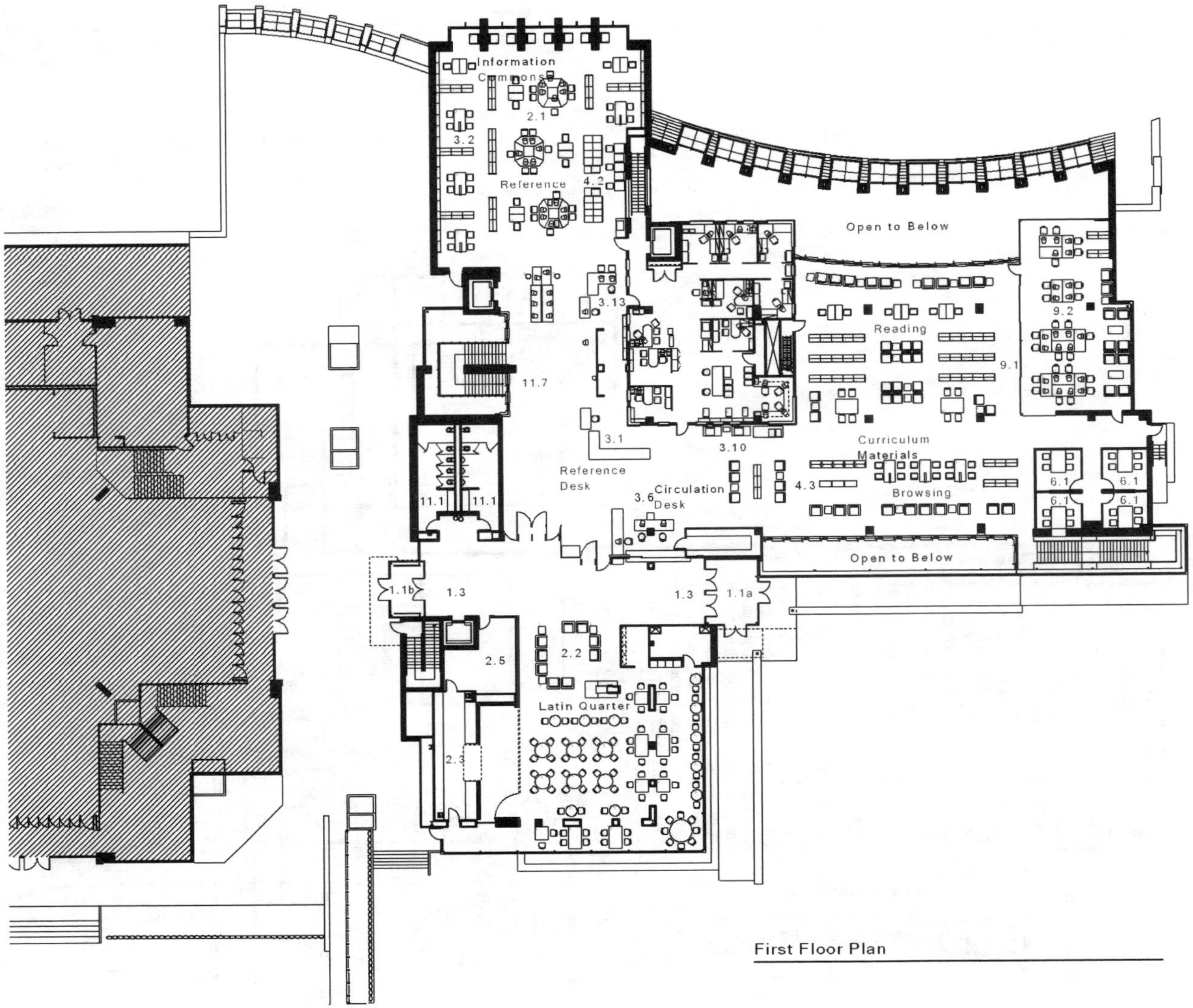

Plan Legend

Introduction to the Library
1.1a Vestibule
1.1b Vestibule
1.2 Building Lobby
1.3 Exit Security Control

Study and Community Areas
2.1 Information Commons
2.2 Latin Quarter
2.3 Latin Quarter Food Service
2.4 Latin Quarter Vending
2.5 Latin Quarter Food Preparation
2.6 Food Storage

Public Services
3.1 Reference Desk
3.2 Reference Collection
3.3 Reference/Circulation Services Workroom
3.4 Reference Services Office
3.5 Public Services Office
3.6 Circulation Desk
3.7 Reserve Shelving
3.8 Circulation Services Office
3.9 Circulation Services Office
3.10 Photocopiers
3.11 Book Drop
3.12 Interlibrary Loan Office
3.13 Help Desk
3.14 Public Service Storage

Library Collections
4.1 General Collection
4.2 Microforms Collection
4.3 Browsing (Periodicals and New Materials)

Archives
5.1 Archives Consultation Room
5.2 Archives Closed Shelf Room

Study Rooms
6.1 Group Study Rooms
6.2 Individual Study Rooms

Technical Services
7.1 Technical Services Workroom
7.2 Technical Services Office
7.3 Technical Services Office
7.4 Technical Services Office
7.5 Technical Services Office
7.6 Technical Services Storage

Administration
8.1 Office of Vice President of AIS
8.2 Administrative Secretary / Receptionist
8.3 Staff Conference Room
8.4 Staff Room
8.5 Staff Office

Instructional Resources
9.1 Curriculum Materials Collection
9.2 Curriculum Materials Computers
9.3 Media Services Office
9.4 Media Services Workroom / Office
9.5 Media Equipment Storage Room
9.6 Editing / Production Rooms
9.7 Production / Presentation Room
9.8 Control Room
9.9 Electronic Classroom
9.10 Writing Center
9.11 Writing Center Office
9.12 Media Services Conference Room

Computer Center
10.1 Computer Center Office
10.2 Computer Center Office
10.3 Computer Center Office
10.4 Computer Center Office
10.5 Computer Center Workroom
10.6 Computer Room
10.7 Computer Storeroom

Non-Assigned Areas
11.1 Toilets
11.2 Janitors Closet
11.3 Mechanical Room
11.4 Electrical Room
11.5 Electrical / Data Closet
11.6 Elevator Machine Room
11.7 Floor Lobby
11.8 Johnson Art Center Deliveries and Holding
11.9 Trash and Recycling Room

FIGURE 7A

First-floor plan, Hedberg Library, Carthage College, Kenosha, Wisconsin. Architects, Meyer, Scherer & Rockcastle, Ltd. Used by permission of the architects. Copyright Meyer, Scherer & Rockcastle, Ltd.

Plan Legend

Introduction to the Library
1.1a Vestibule
1.1b Vestibule
1.2 Building Lobby
1.3 Exit Security Control

Study and Community Areas
2.1 Information Commons
2.2 Latin Quarter
2.3 Latin Quarter Food Service
2.4 Latin Quarter Vending
2.5 Latin Quarter Food Preparation
2.6 Food Storage

Public Services
3.1 Reference Desk
3.2 Reference Collection
3.3 Reference/Circulation Services Workroom
3.4 Reference Services Office
3.5 Public Services Office
3.6 Circulation Desk
3.7 Reserve Shelving
3.8 Circulation Services Office
3.9 Circulation Services Office
3.10 Photocopiers
3.11 Book Drop
3.12 Interlibrary Loan Office
3.13 Help Desk
3.14 Public Service Storage

Library Collections
4.1 General Collection
4.2 Microforms Collection
4.3 Browsing (Periodicals and New Materials)

Archives
5.1 Archives Consultation Room
5.2 Archives Closed Shelf Room

Study Rooms
6.1 Group Study Rooms
6.2 Individual Study Rooms

Technical Services
7.1 Technical Services Workroom
7.2 Technical Services Office
7.3 Technical Services Office
7.4 Technical Services Office
7.5 Technical Services Office
7.6 Technical Services Storage

Administration
8.1 Office of Vice President of AIS
8.2 Administrative Secretary / Receptionist
8.3 Staff Conference Room
8.4 Staff Room
8.5 Staff Office

Instructional Resources
9.1 Curriculum Materials Collection
9.2 Curriculum Materials Computers
9.3 Media Services Office
9.4 Media Services Workroom / Office
9.5 Media Equipment Storage Room
9.6 Editing / Production Rooms
9.7 Production / Presentation Room
9.8 Control Room
9.9 Electronic Classroom
9.10 Writing Center
9.11 Writing Center Office
9.12 Media Services Conference Room

Computer Center
10.1 Computer Center Office
10.2 Computer Center Office
10.3 Computer Center Office
10.4 Computer Center Office
10.5 Computer Center Workroom
10.6 Computer Room
10.7 Computer Storeroom

Non-Assigned Areas
11.1 Toilets
11.2 Janitors Closet
11.3 Mechanical Room
11.4 Electrical Room
11.5 Electrical / Data Closet
11.6 Elevator Machine Room
11.7 Floor Lobby
11.8 Johnson Art Center Deliveries and Holding
11.9 Trash and Recycling Room

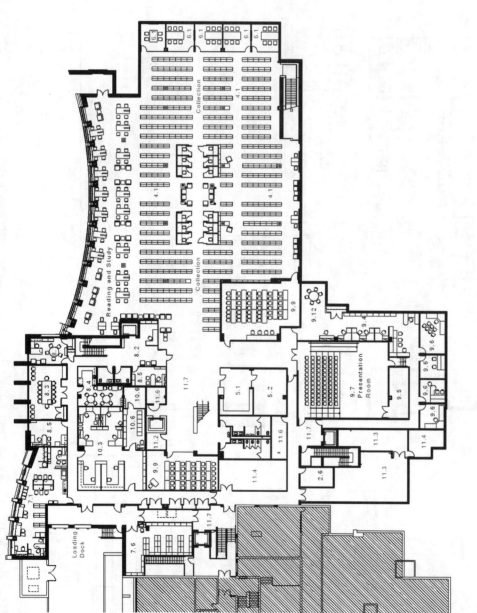

Ground Floor Plan

FIGURE 7B

Ground-floor plan, Hedberg Library, Carthage College, Kenosha, Wisconsin. Architects, Meyer, Scherer & Rockcastle, Ltd. Used by permission of the architects. Copyright Meyer, Scherer & Rockcastle, Ltd.

is at grade. The building is entered through two sets of entrance doors into a lobby on the first floor. A café (referred to as "Latin Quarter" in figure 7A) is entered off the lobby, outside the library space. Rest rooms on this floor are adjacent to the lobby and outside the entrance to the library. Security gates are located at the entrance to the library.

The circulation desk is directly inside the library entrance. The staff expect to implement self-check in the future. An L-shaped reference desk faces both the entrance doors and the corridor to the reference area. A second smaller "help" desk sits next to the reference book collection and the information commons, or main computer area. The work area and offices for circulation, reference, and some automation staff are situated close to the public circulation and reference areas. The remaining areas of the first floor house a browsing area for periodicals and new materials, a special curriculum-materials collection for education students, a reading area, computers to be used in conjunction with the special curriculum collection, and a writing center.

The ground floor of the Hedberg Library houses the general collections of the library, a reading and study area, and individual and group study rooms. Most of the tables in the reading area are equipped with power and data connections. In public libraries, staff members usually offer assistance and maintain visual control on every floor that is open to the public. The Hedberg Library, like many academic libraries, however, does not have staff at service desks on both floors. All of the Hedberg Library's service locations are on the first floor.

Two electronic classrooms and a production/presentation room are on the ground floor of the library. Media-services offices, workroom, storage areas, and editing/production rooms are adjacent to the presentation room. An archives workroom and closed stacks are situated off the lobby. The rest rooms on this floor are inside the library space.

The technical-services and computer-center offices, work areas, and storage are on the ground floor adjacent to the loading dock. The offices of the administrative secretary, the library director, and other staff members are also located on the ground floor. Staff areas on the ground and first floors are internally linked by stairs and an elevator.

Library, River Oaks Baptist School, Houston, Texas; Architects, Kirksey

This library is a 9,000-square-foot facility constructed in 1997. It serves the faculty and 740 students in preschool through the eighth grade. (See figure 8.)

The library has a large open area along one wall, which is enhanced by tall windows. The open area was designed to be used as a storytelling space (with children seated on the carpet) that could serve double-duty by providing an attractive area for school receptions

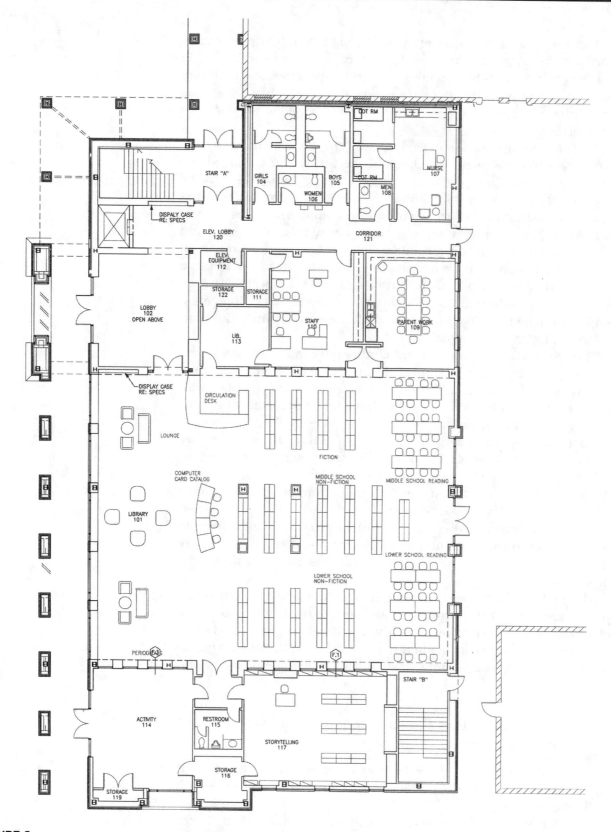

FIGURE 8

Library, River Oaks Baptist School, Houston, Texas. Architects, Kirksey. Used by permission of the architects and River Oaks Baptist School.

when the library is closed for business. (These spaces are indicated as "Lounge" and "Library 101" in figure 8.) The granite-topped circulation desk is the showpiece of the library. The library staff visited other libraries to look at recessed computer monitors in desks and tables. After their visits, they decided to have recessed monitors in the circulation desk and in the computer tables. Because of the availability of electronic resources on networked computers in the classrooms, the library was planned with very few computers for opening day. Later, more computers were added to the library. The large central reading room houses books and magazines on 48"-high shelving for school-age students. The large reading room also includes chairs and tables to accommodate two classes at one time in the library. A smaller room (labeled as "Storytelling" in figure 8) houses the picture and easy book collections.

A small room with a door to the outside (labeled "Activity" in figure 8) was designed as an after-school study area for students. The room is furnished with folding tables and stacking chairs that can be removed or pushed aside to allow for other uses of the room. Since the building opened, the after-hours room has also become home for a special collection of books donated to the library.

The library includes an office for the head librarian and a small work area for the rest of the library staff. The library and the school rely on volunteers who carry out special projects. One small room in the library (labeled "Parent Work" in figure 8) was designed to provide a work area for volunteers and space for housing materials and supplies used for special projects.

Do-It-Yourself Space Planning

Sometimes the staff of public, school, and special libraries do not have the funding needed to hire a design professional to rearrange the library. In that case a do-it-yourself furniture layout is required. You will need a "to-scale" plan of your building (a blueprint), some tracing paper, a ruler, and some tape. If you have a plan scaled to 1/8" = 1'.0" or 1/4" = 1'.0", it is easier to draw the plan using ruled tracing paper with blue lines that will not show when the plan is copied.

Lay your tracing paper over the original blueprint, tape it down, and trace the building footprint with all of the existing walls. Then remove your "new" plan and begin drawing. (If you don't have a scaled plan of the building, you will have to measure and draw one, using a scale of one-quarter or one-eighth inch per one foot of building.)

If you are rearranging existing furnishings, measure each piece, so you will know what dimensions to draw on the plan. Rather than drawing furnishings on a plan, you might cut out scaled furniture shapes and place them in various arrangements on your plan. Begin with an open mind. Start by eliminating the idea that something has to remain where it has always been—including whole areas like the children's space or adult bookstacks. You are just planning on paper—anything goes. You can throw it away and start over.

The following are basic space planning guidelines:

Stack range lengths—usually a maximum of six sections in public libraries.

Double-faced stacks 24" deep; single-faced shelves 12" deep.

Aisles between stacks—minimum 36", 42" preferred; 48" even better.

Guideline for turning space at end of range—48".

Rule of thumb—keep a minimum 36" clear aisle everywhere.

Tables with chairs backing into chairs—5' minimum table edge to table edge.

Consider clear space around a circulation desk for lining up, at reference desks for people waiting, around display racks for people browsing, as well as space for people's feet in lounge areas.

Use your imagination to think about elevations in the interior space. What will you be able to see as you look across a room from a service desk? Consider the location of tall shelves and display racks in relation to service desks.

NOTES

1. Aaron Cohen and Elaine Cohen, *Designing and Space Planning for Libraries: A Behavioral Guide* (New York: R. R. Bowker, 1979), 67.

2. For an extensive discussion of modular construction, see Philip D. Leighton and David C. Weber, *Planning Academic and Research Library Buildings,* 3rd ed. (Chicago: American Library Association, 1999), 424–51.

3. For an extensive discussion of personal space, see Cohen and Cohen, *Designing and Space Planning for Libraries,* 13–20.

4. *ADA Accessibility Guidelines for Buildings and Facilities, Federal Register* 56, no. 144 (July 26, 1991).

Library Furnishings

Because of aesthetic as well as functional concerns, furniture selection is one of the most important aspects of the interior design of a library. The furnishings selected for a library should reflect the overall interior design concept of the building, while serving the functional needs of staff and users.

In small projects with no interior designer, the library staff or board sometimes selects the furnishings. In these projects, the standard offerings of library or commercial furniture manufacturers are usually selected. In large, well-funded projects, some of the furnishings are standard commercial items, while others are designed by architects or interior designers specifically for that library. Custom furnishings are produced by a library or commercial furniture manufacturer or by an architectural woodworking shop. In some projects, an architect, interior designer, or consultant selects standard furnishings and adds special customized features to them. For example, a basic library reading table may be purchased with a custom design on the end panels.

A number of factors affect the cost of purchasing particular furnishings. The price of an item is determined by the volume of items to be purchased; the cost of materials, labor, and finishes; and competition in the marketplace. The larger the quantity of any one kind of item purchased, the lower the price of each item. For example, it is more expensive per unit to buy 10 sections of steel shelving than it is to buy 100 sections. A planning team that decides to buy 25 custom tables this year and 25 of the same tables next year will probably pay more per table than the library that buys all 50 tables at the same time. When all the tables are purchased at one time, the manufacturer has only one factory setup for all 50 tables, prepares a custom finish only one time, buys all of the materials in one order, and ships all of the tables in one truck.

Furniture items used in libraries and other commercial settings are designed to withstand heavy use. The joinery, materials, and hardware are engineered to work together to provide a durable product that will last. The cost of engineering a product must be recovered by a manufacturer when the product is sold. Furnishings offered as standard items by a library company have been previously engineered; the shop drawings required for their manufacture are already available. Standard items are, therefore, less expensive than custom items that have to be designed and engineered prior to production. Because most of the design work has already been done on the item, customized features on a standard product, such as a special end panel on a standard table, do not cost as much as a new custom item.

The amount and kind of materials used in a furniture piece also affect the price. The more solid wood and wood veneers, for example, that are used in an end panel for bookstacks, the higher the price of the end panel will be. An end panel with a 1/8" solid-wood edge band and veneer only on the front of the panel will be less expensive than an end panel with a 2" solid-wood edge band and premium veneer on both faces.

Many library furnishings are made of northern-grown oak because of the availability of that wood. The kind of wood used obviously affects the price of a piece of furniture. Oak furnishings are usually the least expensive, while maple and cherry are slightly more expensive. Special woods, like the highly figured sycamore used in the main library in San Francisco, add to the cost of furnishings. Other special materials, such as stone on the tops and fronts of service desks, also increase the cost of items. The cost of materials is sometimes affected by outside conditions; for example, steel-shelving prices are often based on the cost of steel at a particular time.

Most library furniture manufacturers offer a line of standard color finishes on oak, maple, or other woods. These finishes come at a standard price; however, all of the manufacturers will provide furnishings in a special color finish for an extra cost, called an upcharge. The same is true for steel shelving. All companies have standard colors, but will match other colors for an additional cost.

The cost of furniture is also affected by the market at any given time. A manufacturer who is seeking new projects to increase production at a factory will negotiate or bid lower than a manufacturer with a factory that is working to capacity.

In summary, projects with limited budgets usually purchase standard furniture items with standard finishes; all of the items for the project should be purchased at one time. Projects with large budgets usually have some standard furniture items but also include custom-designed and -engineered furniture items manufactured from special materials with custom finishes.

Members of a library planning team who have not been involved in purchasing furnishings for a new or expanded library need to understand how orders are handled by furniture factories. Some companies, such as manufacturers of office furnishings, have quick-ship programs for specific items; however, most furniture made by large commercial or library furniture manufacturers is produced after the order is received. Factories do not fit a job into the production schedule according to the date the purchaser wants to have the furniture. Orders that require the preparation of shop drawings by the factory and approval of the drawing by the library are usually not placed on the production schedule until the library owner has approved all of the drawings. Orders are placed on the production schedule, therefore, in the order in which they are received and any required shop drawings are completed. The delivery date of furnishings depends on a number of variables, some controlled by the manufacturer and some controlled by the library owner. Some of these factors include the following:

The length of time the factory takes to produce the shop drawings

The length of time the owner takes to approve and return approved shop drawings to the factory

The availability of the materials required for producing the furnishings

The length of time the factory requires to prepare finish or product samples

The length of time the owner takes to approve and return approved finish or product samples to the factory

The number of jobs already in the production schedule queue at the factory

The changes required by the owner after the job is in production (for example, the building construction may fall behind schedule)

The interior designer, consultant, or (on small projects) the librarian continues to coordinate the schedule of building construction and the delivery dates of the furniture throughout the furnishings production period. Because so many variables are involved, it is difficult to determine the exact date that furnishings will all be delivered and installed. Standard steel shelving and office furnishings may be delivered two to three months after the factory receives a purchase order. On small projects, wood furniture items that are mostly standard pieces may be produced in three to four months. Larger projects with many custom-designed furnishings may require four to six months (or longer) to produce.

The cost of a piece of durable commercial furniture is often higher than the cost of a piece of residential furniture. The difference in price should be justified to reluctant funding bodies by using the concept of life-cycle costing. The life-cycle price is the cost of a piece of furniture with the number of years the item will last factored in.

Service Desks

All types of libraries have service desks. In small school and public libraries, and in some special libraries, one desk serves both circulation and reference functions. (See figures 9 and 10.) In larger academic and public libraries, users may receive service at several different desks designed for circulation functions and several other desks designed for reference and information functions. In large libraries, some staff may answer traditional reference questions from behind a service desk, while other staff or docents roam among computer workstations assisting people with questions. In a multistory library, users can more easily locate a service desk when each desk is placed in the same relative location on each floor. Service points can be more easily identified by users if all of the desks are designed with the same materials, finishes, or colors.

FIGURE 9

Springhill Elementary School, Longview, Texas. Jeff Potter Architects. Concertina desk manufactured by BCI. Photo used by permission of Libra-Tech Corporation. Photo credit: Penny Schmitz.

FIGURE 10

Beeville Public Library, Beeville, Texas. Ray Bailey Architects. Photo used by permission of the photographers. Photo credit: Copyright Hester & Hardaway-Photographers.

In most small to medium-sized public libraries, check-in and check-out of materials is handled at one desk located near the entrance to the library. These desks are often custom-designed, monumental pieces of architectural woodwork meant to serve as the centerpiece of the library's interior. In recent years, some libraries have preferred to install modular desks with components that, theoretically, can be rearranged or added to as library needs change. In larger libraries, circulation functions may be handled at multiple desks, with one for check-out, another for check-in, and a third for reserved items.

Another alternative to the single circulation desk is based on the concept of check-out counters in a retail store. Instead of one large circulation desk where several staff members serve the public, smaller, separate circulation stations serve individual lines of users, like the check-out stands at a grocery store. Individual circulation stations help to define where people wait in line for service and to indicate who is the next person to be served.

Service desks are built in many shapes and sizes. (See figure 11.) Some desks are designed with a stairstep design across the face to delineate separate check-in and check-out stations. Desks are square, rectangular, or round in shape. A curved desk works if the desk is large and designed to accommodate four or more staff at one time. Small round desks do not function well, however, because staff members tend to get in each other's way as they are working.

Service desks may be considered pieces of millwork that are included in the construction contract, or they may be considered furniture items and included in the furniture package. Desks may be built by millwork houses, by library furniture manufacturers, or by architectural woodworking companies. Sometimes the outer shell of

FIGURE 11

Harold B. Lee Library, Brigham Young University, Provo, Utah. Reference desk, tables, chairs, paneling, and trim manufactured by Fetzers' Inc. Photo used by permission of Fetzers' Inc. Photo credit: Douglas Kahn.

a desk is constructed by a millwork house and the interior components are made by a furniture manufacturer. This sounds possible in theory, but it is difficult to coordinate two sets of shop drawings and the installation for both pieces and have the two portions of the desk work together perfectly when both are installed.

Architects should be asked to set aside any preconceived ideas that they have about the manufacture of service desks and to work with the local planning team to determine the best options for the library. Architects should review, with the planning team, the pros and cons of using a millwork desk as opposed to a manufactured desk.

Regardless of how desks are purchased and manufactured, thorough planning is essential for each individual library and situation. When a new library is planned, the local planning team should work closely with the architect and other design professionals to make sure that many options in regard to the design and manufacture of the desk are considered. The basic requirements for a desk should be included in the building program: number of separate desks required for circulation and reference, type of desks (traditional desks or individual check-out stations), maximum number of staff to be accommodated, maximum number of computers and other equipment to be used, types of storage needed (shelves; box, pencil, and file drawers; slots; specialty shelves), operations to occur (check-in, check-out, reference assistance, materials' return, borrower registrations, reserved items pick-up), special requirements, and the ages or capabilities of the users who will approach the desk. (See figure 12.) The building program should also note any items to be located directly behind the desk, such as ready-reference books on shelves or book trucks, and how much space will be needed to accommodate these items.

FIGURE 12

Davis Library, Plano, Texas. Architects, Phillips Swager Associates. Photo used by permission of the photographer. Photo credit: Copyright King Graf 2001.

The building program should state any requirements for access to and egress from the desk by the staff. In libraries with theft-detection systems, it is sometimes necessary for staff to be able to exit easily and quickly from behind the desk when the system alarm sounds.

Some of the issues to be addressed in the building program will be based on the policies and procedures of the library. For example, the staff at the desk may be expected to stand or to sit on high stools at all times, in order to be at eye level for all users approaching the desk. Or the staff may be allowed to be at seated height until someone approaches. The design of a desk may be determined by the clientele of the library and the types of questions that will be asked. In an academic or medical library, for example, questions may require a long consultation between the library staff and the user. In this case, both staff and user may wish to be seated on the same side of the desk so each can view the same computer with ease. A need for privacy in conducting reference interviews may also be a consideration in designing the configuration of a service desk.

Library staff should be closely involved in designing the interior components of a desk. The architect or interior designer should interview staff who will be using the desk and ask them to state their needs and expectations for the desk. Following the interview, a design professional should prepare a simple drawing of the interior of the desk that provides his or her interpretation of staff requirements. The staff should then be asked to review the drawing. The staff and the designer should work together until they agree on a satisfactory configuration of interior desk components. In large projects, a mock-up of the proposed desk may be built to ensure that the finished desk will fulfill the requirements of the staff and the library users.

The exterior of the desk is designed by the architect or interior designer, but with review and approval by the local planning team. The standard height of the worksurface of a circulation desk is 39". This is a time-tested standard—36" is too low for a tall person and 42" is too high for a short person. Design professionals are urged not to deviate from this height.

ADA guidelines require that one unit of each service counter must be accessible from a wheelchair. The unit must be located on an accessible route and must be at least 36" wide. The unit can have a maximum height of 36" from the finished floor, if the accessible area is designed for a library user in a wheelchair to pull alongside the desk. Other ADA guidelines suggest that a unit designed to allow a user in a wheelchair to pull under the desktop should have a worksurface between 28" and 34" above the finished floor. In situations where the wheelchair is pulled under the desktop, kneespace that is a minimum of 19" deep must be provided.

One 36"-wide accessible unit, 30" deep, is not sufficient in a library where the staff wish to sit facing a person in a wheelchair who has pulled under the desk. A 30"-deep worksurface will not allow for the 19" of knee space required of a person in a wheelchair in addition to adequate knee space for a library employee seated directly opposite on the staff side of the desk. If two 36"-wide units are used for the ADA-required unit, the wheelchair user can pull up under one 36" portion of the desk and the staff member can sit comfortably pulled up under the other 36" portion of the desk. Equipment can be arranged in such a manner that a computer does not obscure the line of sight between the user and the staff member.

For many years, the standard depth for circulation desks manufactured by library furniture companies was 30". As computer equipment grew larger, however, the 30" depth became too narrow to accommodate the equipment, unless a pullout keyboard tray was also used. Service desktops had to be increased to 36" or 38" deep in order to accommodate a monitor, a keyboard, and grommet holes for dropping cords beneath the top (except in situations where flat-screen or recessed monitors are used).

In determining the depth of a service desk, the following should be considered:

A need for relative privacy in conducting circulation and reference transactions. The two people involved in the transaction should be close enough to use low voices while speaking to each other across the desk.

Attitudes about personal space. The two people in the transaction should be about three feet apart in order to feel comfortable with each other.

At a circulation desk, the desk should be narrow enough for users and staff to push stacks of books across the desktop for checkout—the desk should be no deeper than an arm's length.

The desk should be deep enough to accommodate all of the equipment that will be placed there, while still maintaining adequate personal space for staff and users.

Usually the design of a custom desk has an impact on the depth of the desk. For example, when a reference desk is designed with a transaction counter around the staff side, the transaction counter cannot intrude so far over the staff worksurface of the desk that the staff's usable portion of the desk is not deep enough to accommodate computer equipment.

In a library expecting a high volume of circulation, a transaction top on a circulation desk (a counter higher than the rest of the worksurface) is not recommended. It is easier for staff to push a stack of checked-out materials across a desktop to the user than to pick up the stack of materials and lift them to the higher level of the transaction top. At a reference desk, however, the staff worksurface may be at 29" high, while the desk has a transaction counter at 36" high. The transaction counter is convenient because a reference book can be placed on the counter to be viewed by a user and a staff member.

The basic units of custom service desks are constructed of wood that is faced with a variety of materials, including wood veneer, high-pressure plastic laminate, steel, and stone. The tops of desks are faced with laminate, granite, marble, or synthetic materials such as Corian and Granirex. When laminate tops are used on a desk, all edges of the desk should be banded with solid wood to prevent damage to the laminate. Laminate tops that are self-edged are not recommended for any desk; the edges can be easily chipped when staff or users bump into them with a book or other object. Granite or marble tops are often used for aesthetic purposes; however, stone tops should be considered for functional reasons also. The color in plastic laminate tops eventually wears away as a result of pushing books across the top of a circulation desk, so the top must be replaced. Stone tops last for the life of the library and are recommended for academic and public libraries where extensive use is expected. The use of synthetic materials, such as Corian, for desktops should be considered carefully. Some materials may contract over time and leave gaps in the desktop between sections of the material.

One of the most important aspects of planning service desks involves determining how power, data, and wire management will be handled in a desk. Power, data, and telephones may be accessed at the desktop from floor outlets installed under the desk or from outlets installed inside the desk on the staff side. Outlets must be carefully placed so that they are as far away as possible from the feet of staff working at the desk. Enough outlets and circuits must be provided to handle the maximum number of computers and other equipment expected to be used for the lifetime of the desk. Electrical outlets that are a fixed part of the building are inflexible and cannot be moved easily.

Desks made by library-furniture manufacturers are often purchased with three- or four-circuit, eight-wire, integrated electrical systems that are installed along the length of the desk. Outlets for data and power are located below the top of the desk. The electrical system is hardwired to the building power at one point, where the electrical contractor for the building has supplied a junction box with appropriate wires. Flexibility is an advantage to a built-in system; power is supplied along the length of the desk and outlets can be moved or added as the placement of equipment on the desktop changes. The integrated electrical systems in library furniture are similar to the systems that are used to power office-panel systems. Architects and designers who are not familiar with library furnishings are encouraged to consider all of the ways of handling power and data in service desks prior to making specific plans.

Cords and cables from equipment housed on top of the desk are passed through the top to the area below the surface by means of grommet holes. Grommets are often a problem. In many cases, holes for dropping cords are drilled into the desktop on-site when the desk is installed. Grommet sleeves are placed in the holes; covers are placed over the holes that are not being used presently. Unfortunately, the covers are sometimes pulled out by people waiting at the desk and are subsequently lost. The open holes are unsightly, and inappropriate items are dropped through them. So-called tamper-proof grommets have covers that are controlled by a spring, but eventually the spring will fail to work. Most libraries need grommets that are a minimum of 3" in diameter or rectangular grommets that are even larger. Consult with the library's technology staff to determine the size and location of grommets needed.

Wire management is an issue related to the increased use of electronic equipment. Ideally, all of the cords and cables below the desktop would be stashed neatly in wire-management trays, so that a staff member working behind the desk would not see a mess of cords beneath the desktop. Library-furniture manufacturers supply wire-management channels that are installed along the length of the desk; however, the channels are often too small to accommodate the massive amount of cords, cables, and transformers that are housed below the desktop. Also, the furniture supplier may manage to place all of the cords in the wire-management channels when the desk is first installed, but as equipment changes, library staff do not take the time to get down on their hands and knees and attempt to maneuver the cords into the undersized wire-management channel.

The author worked with the Worden Company to devise a mesh bag for wire management that has worked successfully at the Sugar Land Branch of the Fort Bend County Libraries, in Sugar Land, Texas. The bag is attached to the underside of a desk or a tabletop. The top of the bag is held shut with Velcro. When the top is opened, all of the cords can be easily placed in the flexible bag. The bag has holes in the sides for stringing cords from bag to bag, if necessary. The bag is large enough to hold more cords than any rigid wire-management channel now available.

The mess of cords under a service desk can also be hidden by constructing a second, inside wall, or panel, in the desk. The panels serve to hide the cords and power and data entries. The panels are equipped with doors to allow the staff to access power and data equipment when needed.

The view of the backs of computers and multiple cords is an unattractive part of circulation desks. The exposed cords are also a problem where young children are able to reach and pull the cords. While a transaction top helps to hide the backs of computers, the ergonomic risk to staff, caused by lifting books from one desk level to another, outweighs the aesthetic benefits. Permanent screens or wells to partially hide computers can be built into a circulation desk, but they limit the use of computers along the worksurface—computers can only be used where screens or wells have been constructed. Movable screens can be designed to match the desk and can be attached with Velcro tape to the desk. Flat-screen monitors used at a circulation desk are a much more attractive option than bulky CRTs.

Another solution for eliminating an unsightly view of the back of computers is the use of recessed monitors. Recessed monitors are placed in a "cradle" mounted under the worksurface of the desk. The monitor is viewed through a piece of glass that is flush with the desktop. The mechanism for recessed monitors is available from several manufacturers, such as Nova and Parallax, and can be mounted into any custom desk. (Desks for recessed monitors are available as standard furniture items supplied by several manufacturers.) Staff are usually not accustomed to using recessed monitors. Before specifying recessed monitors for a library, therefore, it is a good idea to give staff an opportunity to visit a library where such monitors are used at a service desk. Make sure everyone can see the screen. Some people with bifocals may find it difficult to adjust to viewing a recessed screen. Another disadvantage of recessed monitors is that staff cannot show a screen to a user requesting to see a record.

In plans for the arrangement of modules within a circulation desk, functions should move from left to right (from the public point of view), with the return of items and check-in on the left side of the desk and check-out on the right side. A book-return unit should be located in the area closest to the main entrance to the library, so that people can return materials as soon as they enter the building.

On some projects, architects provide detailed drawings of service desks that are used for the purpose of bidding. The drawings are part of the construction drawings, if the desk is a millwork item, or are part of the furniture bid document, if the desks are purchased as part of the furniture bid.

In some small projects, the service desks are described in the furniture bid specifications and illustrated only with diagrams. The following is a sample specification for a two-part reference desk. The specification illustrates the kinds of detailed decisions that must be made when designing a desk (even apart from the actual construction of the desk). The details on the front of the desk described here match details on the library's circulation desk. Three drawings accompanied the specification in the bid document. (See plates 3A and 3B.)

> The desk shall be faced on all exposed surfaces with cherry veneers. The patron side of both sections of the desk shall be faced with cherry veneer, with hickory veneer inlays to match the circulation desk design.
>
> A transaction top on the front section of the reference desk shall be supplied with a 3/4" Granirex slab top with an ogee bullnose edge on all edges. The top of the back section of the desk shall be supplied with a 3/4"-thick Granirex slab top with an ogee bullnose edge on the patron side of the desk and a bullnose edge on the staff side. The 29"-high worksurface on the front unit shall be laminate with 5/16"-thick solid cherry edge band.
>
> Both sections of the desk shall be supplied on both the patron and staff sides with a 6"-high toe kick, recessed 3". The toe kick shall be constructed of 3/4" unfinished plywood. Porcelain tile supplied by the Construction Contractor will be applied on-site by the tile

setter, under the direction of the Architect. The vendor awarded the bid for the desk shall be responsible for supplying and installing all parts of the desk, including the Granirex top.

The overall depth of the desk on the front section, including the transaction top, shall be 38". The back section of the desk shall be 36" deep. The desk shall have a transaction top approximately 9" deep that shall extend around all modules of the front section of the desk (but not around the end panels). The transaction top shall extend approximately 2" beyond the front edge of the desk and approximately 7" over the 29"-high worksurface. Support for the transaction top shall be on the working side of the desk and shall be hidden from public view. The transaction top shall be designed to allow for clear space on the work surface of 28". A cord-drop slot shall be located in the space under the transaction top. The slot shall begin at least 28" from the working-side edge of the top.

Two power-entry devices shall be supplied to the integrated electrical system—one power entry for each part of the desk. The reference desk shall have the same electrical specifications as the General Electrical Specifications.

The desk shall have the same construction specifications as the circulation desk.

The front section of the desk shall be supplied with the following modules:

> *Module A:* 36" wide × nominal 38" deep × 29" high at worksurface. Shelf unit supplied with one adjustable shelf and one fixed base shelf.
>
> *Module B:* Curved, closed corner unit. Supply closed-access panel through one side of the corner unit to allow for maneuvering data cables through the corner unit.
>
> *Module C:* 36" wide × nominal 38" deep × 29" high at worksurface. Knee-space unit with no fixed base.
>
> *Module D:* 36" wide × nominal 38" deep × 29" high at worksurface. Storage unit with two drawers, 6" high × 18" wide at the top of the unit and one fixed base shelf.
>
> *Module E:* 36" wide × nominal 38" deep × 29" high at worksurface. Knee-space unit with no fixed base.
>
> *Module F:* Curved, closed corner unit. Supply closed-access panel through one side of the corner unit to allow for maneuvering data cables through the corner unit.

Module G: 36" wide × nominal 38" deep × 29" high at worksurface. Shelf unit supplied with one adjustable shelf and one fixed base shelf.

The back section of the desk shall be supplied with the following modules:

Module H: 36" wide × 36" deep × 36" high. Closed cabinet unit. Fixed base with two doors that open out from the center of the unit. Supply interior of cabinet with two adjustable shelves.

Module I: Curved, closed corner unit. Supply closed-access panel through one side of the corner unit to allow for maneuvering data cables through the corner unit.

Module J: Nominal 36" wide × 36" deep × 36" high. Atlas case with access from the patron side of the desk. Atlas case shall have five pullout shelves operating on full-extension ball-bearing slides, with stops to prevent removal. Each shelf shall have a clear area of 26" wide × 24-1/2" deep × 3-3/8" high. Shelves shall be constructed of 3/4"-thick plywood with cherry face and 1-1/2"–wide front retainer. The staff side of the atlas unit shall be faced with cherry veneer.

Module K: Nominal 72" wide × 36" deep × 36" high. Shelving unit built with access to nominal 18"-deep shelves on the patron side and nominal 18"-deep shelves on the staff side. Full back panel between the two shelving sides of the unit. Each shelving unit on both sides shall be supplied with a fixed base shelf and two adjustable shelves. Units shall have standard wood library shelving construction with intermediate panel.

Module L: Curved, closed corner unit. Supply closed-access panel through one side of the corner unit to allow for maneuvering data cables through the corner unit.

Module M: 36" wide × 36" deep × 36" high. Storage unit with four legal-sized file cabinets and a fixed base.

Supply two end panels 29" high for the front section of the desk and two end panels 36" high for the back section of the desk.

Some libraries are installing self-check machines in the library or are including access to power and data for the future use of self-check equipment. In selecting a location for self-check, keep in mind that patrons may need some instructions the first time they use the equipment, so the machine should be placed within a short distance from a service desk. On the other hand, the self-check equipment should not be so close to the check-out desk that people waiting to use self-check get in the way of others in line to check out books by the traditional method. Self-check machines may be used successfully in a children's area, where young people learn how to use the equipment quickly.

Shelving

Over the last few years, new libraries have included a larger amount of interior public space devoted to computers in proportion to space used for bookstacks. Except in a few academic libraries, however, shelving units for housing books and audiovisual materials have remained an essential part of the furnishings for any library. Standard library shelving consists of three-foot sections of shelving placed together to form ranges of shelving. In some situations, sections of shelving that are 24" or 30" wide are used.

Architects and interior designers who are considering providing lights on bookstacks rather than general lighting in a stack area should study the possibility carefully and discuss the idea with the local planning team. The flexibility of a library interior is essential because of the kinds of changes occurring in libraries in general. The use of only stack lighting severely restricts the rearrangement of the stacks. If stacks are removed from an area, general lighting must be added later, when funds may not be available. If stack lighting is used for aesthetic reasons or to improve the visibility of the stacks, general lighting that is adequate for future use of the space without the stack lighting should also be installed in the area.

Wood shelving or architectural woodwork is often used in small special libraries where the aesthetic look of wood is an important aspect of the interior design of the space. Designers who are considering the use of wood shelving should read an article by Ann Massman entitled "The Wood Shelving Dilemma."[1] The article outlines the ways in which wood shelving puts library materials at risk of damage because of its acidic nature and other chemical components in wood. Massman states that "it is strongly recommended not to use wood shelving and other wood storage equipment to store library materials with long-term value."

Most libraries are furnished with steel cantilevered shelving, which is less expensive and provides more flexibility for changing out the components than wood shelving. Architects and interior designers who have not planned libraries for several years are urged to tour the exhibits at a library conference or talk to local vendors about shelving products currently on the market.

The safety of steel bookstacks was an issue in the past, when most shelving units were starter/adder systems that depended on sway braces with turnbuckles for stability. Architects and others specifying steel shelving now benefit from the independent performance-testing of steel bookstacks carried out under the auspices of the staff of *Library Technology Reports* during the 1990s. In order to ensure that shelving purchased meets the highest performance standards, specifications for steel bookstacks should require that shelving shall have been tested and shall have passed the standards set by ANSI/NISO Z39.73 1994, "Single-Tier Steel Bracket Library Shelving." The standards ensure that the shelving bears prescribed loads without sagging or bending, that the shelving finish endures normal use for at least 30 years, and that changing the position of adjustable shelves can be accomplished without tools.

Decisions regarding the details of shelving to be purchased should be discussed by the design professionals with the library staff. What is desired in one library may not be what is needed in another. The first decision to be made is whether to use wood or steel shelving. Some libraries use steel shelving in most of the library, but use wood shelving or architectural woodwork in rooms for special collections or local history.[2]

Before making final decisions about shelving, the following issues and questions regarding steel shelving should be addressed. The items listed are relevant to all types of libraries.

Types of Steel Shelving

Most libraries today purchase one of two types of shelving, either welded-frame systems or European-style starter/adder systems. Products of both types have passed the required performance testing. Welded-frame systems consist of uprights and spreaders that are welded together; each section of shelving includes a four-sided frame. With welded-frame shelving, all frames are alike; a starter section is not needed at the end of each range.

European starter/adder shelving, introduced into the United States by the Danish company BCI, consists of a T-base welded to an upright. Top and bottom spreaders are attached to the uprights with a hook-in type of assembly. Some systems add a center crossbar to every three to five sections for stability. Because of the attractive rectangular shelf brackets on starter/adder shelving, this type of shelving is sometimes used without end panels.

Either type of shelving is acceptable. Sometimes the welded-frame systems are slightly less expensive than starter/adder systems. In an open-bid situation, where the library wants the best price regardless of which type of shelving is used, manufacturers of both types of systems could be listed as acceptable and the specifications written to allow vendors of both products to bid.

Several shelving manufacturers also offer special systems designed for highlighting special collections. Some public libraries use these specialty systems, like BCI's System Arc, for displaying new books and audiovisual materials near the library entrance. These and other shelving systems can be equipped with lights. The use of lighted shelving must be planned, of course, at the same time as the electrical plans for the building are determined.

Heights of Shelving

Decisions regarding the height of shelving to be specified depend on how the bookstacks will be used. In children's areas of public libraries, for example, picture-book shelving for preschoolers should be no more than 42" high, while shelving for school-age children may be 48" or 66" high. In elementary school libraries, where space is available, the staff may prefer to have no shelving higher than 48". In academic libraries, where the most efficient use of space is the prime consideration, 90" stacks will be used. Because of the size of the volumes, shelving in law libraries may be as high as 93".

In many libraries, the height of the shelving may be determined by a need for visual control from a service desk to the other side of a reading room. Where line of sight is a priority, shelving should be no more than 42" high. In the adult areas of public libraries, shelving heights may vary because of the height of the ceiling, the types of materials to be housed, and the amount of overall space available for shelving the collection. Where space is limited, collections are usually placed on shelving 90" high. Because of the difficulty of retrieving books from the top shelf of a 90"-high stack, most public libraries would prefer to have shelving for adults that is 78" or 84" high. Some libraries place nonfiction on 90" shelves, but place fiction, large-print books, and audiovisual collections on lower shelves, such as 78" or 66" high.

Wall and Freestanding Shelving

Steel shelving is available as single-faced or double-faced sections. Single-faced shelving must be attached to a wall for stability. Double-faced shelving is often freestanding. In many libraries, double-faced stacks do not need to be attached to the floor, and no special bracing is required. Libraries in earthquake-prone areas should be familiar with their governmental requirements for the installation of library shelving where double-faced shelving must be permanently attached to the floor or braced overhead.

Shelves

Standard adjustable shelves are available in many different depths; for example, 8", 9", 10", 12", and 16". Some specialty shelves are only 6" deep. The shelf depth needed depends on the type of material to be housed on the shelf. Specialty shelves for audiovisual materials are usually 6" or 8" deep. Books for school-age children and adult fiction will fit on a 10" shelf. Most picture books, adult nonfiction, and reference book shelving should be 12" deep. Law books may require shelves 14" or 16" deep.

In specifying shelves, it is important to discuss with vendors, and to indicate in your specifications, whether the depth of the shelves you are ordering is actual or nominal. Some vendors discuss shelves in terms of nominal depth, that is, the depth of the *actual* steel shelf may be one inch less than the *nominal* depth. On a regular flat shelf with no back, the nominal depth is the depth from the front edge of the shelf to the imaginary centerline of the shelving frame. In other words, the vendor may be including the space at the back of the shelf created by the upright as part of the depth of the shelf.

Adjustable shelves may be regular flat shelves that allow for pushing a book back beyond the actual depth of the shelf, or the adjustable shelves may have an integral back (an upturned flange about 1" to 1-1/2" high) that prevents books from moving beyond the actual back of the shelf. If the library intends to use a sliding book support, integral shelves are required.

In some shelving systems, each side of a double-faced section of shelving has a separate base shelf. In other systems, the base shelf is double-faced, and only one shelf is specified. Base shelves that slope up are available and are popular in public libraries. The slope helps to make titles on the bottom shelf more visible. Base shelves are available in the same sizes as adjustable shelves. Many libraries specify the base shelf deeper than the adjustable shelves in order to increase stability. For example, if 10"-deep shelves are specified on sections of wall shelving, a 12"-deep base may be specified. A vendor would refer to this shelving as "10 over 12."

Special Shelving Components

Picture-book shelving for children's areas has 12"-deep shelves that are supplied with a full back. The shelves are slotted to accommodate movable dividers to hold the books upright. Five dividers per shelf, including the base shelf, should be specified. Similar slotted shelves can also be used for housing back issues of magazines or small books, such as plays or *Cliff's Notes.*

All shelving systems offer periodical display units with fixed or hinged shelves. Hinged periodical shelves can be fitted with a slotted shelf beneath the display unit for the storage of recent back issues of magazines. Current issues of newspapers can be displayed on periodical display units fitted with one- or two-piece hinged Plexiglas covers.

All shelving systems offer a wide variety of special shelves for audiovisual and other materials. Shelves to hold CDs, paperbacks, videos, and DVDs are 6" to 8" deep and are sloped up to hold the materials in place. These shelves may be ordered with or without slots and dividers. Other accessories include a rod that fits into the shelving frame to hold hanging bags (for children's books and cassettes, for example), browser boxes that fit into shelving frames for audiovisual materials or paperbacks, and pullout reference shelves located where users may need to set down a book and open it in the stacks.

It would be helpful if one type of book support could be recommended, but the perfect book support that will satisfy everyone has yet to be invented. Some librarians are proponents of sliding book supports on integral back shelves, while others say the sliding book supports don't really slide and the plastic brackets break easily. The type of wire book support that is squeezed to fit under the shelf above may work if the books are tall enough to fit behind the book support, the tension on the support is strong enough, and the gauge of wire is sufficient. For many years, the Houston Public Library bought Gaylord's large, cork-based book supports and had them finished to match the shelving purchased. The staff there felt this was the best book support. For length of years of satisfactory service, a 9"-tall, findable book support with a cork base may be the easiest way to go.

If sliding or wire book supports are to be purchased, ask for several to try out before purchase. Try them out on full shelves of books of various heights. In a bid situation, require bidders to supply sample book supports to be tested on-site.

Canopy Tops and End Panels

Steel shelving can be purchased with matching steel canopy tops that should match the depth of the base of the shelving. In situations where money is an issue and aesthetics is of less importance than function, 90"-high shelving can be used without canopy tops. Without the tops, some librarians say the titles on the volumes on the top shelves can be viewed more easily because the tops don't block light from above.

Most public libraries prefer canopy tops because they give the shelving a more finished appearance. Steel tops are not very functional for low shelving where items will be placed for display. The paint gets marred and the tops can bend with the weight of some objects. In many cases, shelving that is 42" and 48" high is specified with custom tops that are made of particleboard faced and self-edged with laminate, faced with laminate and edged with solid wood bands, or faced with wood veneer and edged with solid wood bands. Low shelving may also have granite or marble tops. In a bidding situation, the shelving supplier and the manufacturer of the custom tops should be required to work together to ensure that the tops fit the specific shelving supplied. The bid document should also indicate whether the shelving vendor or the custom-top vendor will supply the hardware for attaching the tops. In some projects, the architect or the interior designer may design special stone tops, cornice tops, or wood bases, in order to give steel shelving a less utilitarian look.

In large academic libraries where ranges of stacks are purely functional, steel shelving may be purchased without end panels. Likewise, some public libraries using the European-style starter/adder shelving may choose not to use end panels. Most libraries, however, choose to use some type of end panel. The least expensive ones are matching steel end panels purchased along with the shelving system. The cost of end panels varies greatly, depending on the type of materials used, the size of the end panels, and the custom detail specified. End panels are made with particleboard or lumber cores that are faced in some manner. (See figures 13, 14, and 15.) The following are some end-panel options:

End panels with laminate on both faces and all edges.

End panels with laminate face on both sides and with a solid wood edge around all four sides of the panel. The solid wood edge may have one of many different shapes.

End panels with slat wall on the outer face, laminate on the backside, and all sides self-edged with laminate.

FIGURE 13

Mira Mesa Branch Library, Mira Mesa, California. Architects, BSHA. Used by permission of MJ Industries. Photo credit: Don Snipes Photography.

End panels with slat wall on the outer face, laminate on the backside, and with a solid wood edge around all four sides. (Slat walls can be supplied with no inserts, or with plastic or aluminum inserts between the slats.)

End panels with wood-veneer face on both sides and solid wood edge band on four sides. The price of wooden end panels depends on the thickness of the panel (the thicker it is, the more expensive), the size and shape of the solid wood edge (the wider it is, the more expensive), and detailing at the corners.

End panels with wood-veneer face on both sides and solid wood edge band on four sides and with special custom details added; for example, laser-cut drawers, special inlays, details added to match other furnishings, and details designed to accommodate end panel signs.

FIGURE 14
Loudoun County Public Library, Leesburg, Virginia. Used by permission of MJ Industries. Photo credit: Paul Colburn.

In order to meet a budget on a small project, it may be necessary to work with a vendor to determine how the library can afford wooden end panels. For example, a vendor may begin by quoting you a price for a wooden end panel that is 1-3/8" thick with a 5/8" solid wood edge around all four sides. Instead, ask for a quote on a panel that is 3/4" thick and that has a 1/8" strip of solid wood around the outside edges.

The same end panel need not be used in all parts of the library. Detailed custom panels may be used near the entrance to the library to make a good first impression, while less fancy end panels may be used in other parts of the library. It is not uncommon for the children's area of a public library to have end panels entirely different from the adult part of the library. The end panels in a children's area

FIGURE 15

Berlin Peck Memorial Library, Berlin, Connecticut. Used by permission of MJ Industries. Photo credit: Hutchins Photography, Inc.

offer architects and interior designers an opportunity to display their creativity. The end panels in the children's area may be faced with several different colors of laminate. Wood end panels may be decorated with laser-cut images of interest to children. (See figure 16.)

Computer Furniture

Almost any worksurface in a library carries the potential for becoming furniture to hold a computer at some point in the life cycle of the library. During the design process for new and renovated libraries, however, specific pieces of furniture are purchased to hold computers for library users and staff.

All library-furniture manufacturers offer some type of standard computer furniture that can be easily customized to fit the requirements of a particular library. The following are some of the questions to be asked in designing or selecting computer furniture.

What kind of work will library users be doing at the computer? Will people use it to make quick catalog searches, or will they spend a longer time researching topics on the Internet and other electronic resources? Will furniture be needed for self-check machines now or in the future?

Who will be using the computer? Will it be used by preschoolers and school-age children playing educational games? By medical school students researching a topic? By high school students doing a homework assignment?

How many people will be using the computer at one time? Will single individuals use each computer all of the time, or will two or three people use the computer collaboratively?

How much equipment is each computer workstation expected to hold? Monitor, keyboard, and CPU only? A printer? Speakers? A scanner?

How will the interface between the computers and building power and data be accomplished?

Quick catalog searches can be done at a computer placed on a stand-up table with a 39"-high worksurface. Most libraries need fewer stand-up computers and more computers at lower heights. Longer computer searches require a sit-down table with a worksurface that is 29" high. (See figures 17 and 18.)

Computers used for a quick catalog search can be accommodated on a worksurface that is 36" wide. Computers used for longer transactions require surfaces 48" to 60" wide, so that the person using the computer has space for books and papers beside the equipment. Also, greater privacy for each person is afforded by a wider worksurface for each computer.

Most libraries need workstations designed to accommodate more than one person using a single computer. Students at all levels, children, and even adults sometimes work collaboratively at a computer for particular projects. Homework assignments sometimes require working together at one computer. Preschoolers often use a computer with a parent or caregiver. Use of a single computer by several young teenagers is frequently an after-school social activity in public libraries. Sometimes an entire family may become involved in using a computer.

Collaborative use of computers has implications for the size, configuration, and location of computers in the library. The amount of space allocated for each computer on a table should be large enough

FIGURE 17

Hudsonville High School, Hudsonville, Michigan. De Gilde computer table manufactured by the Worden Company. Used by permission of the Worden Company.

(48" to 60" wide) to allow more than one person to view the computer screen at the same time. Stools or chairs for two or three children and adults should be provided for every computer in the children's department of a public library. In academic libraries where collaborative learning is expected, large six-sided computer workstations that allow for several people to sit close to the computer are sometimes used. The furniture usually has tall dividers between each piece of the "pie" to give each group some privacy.

The collaborative use of computers can be a noisy activity. Some individuals in public libraries like to use a computer in a relatively quiet area with little conversation going on around them. Some accommodation may be made for these users by placing some of the workstations away from the area where most of the collaborative activity is going on.

Decisions regarding computer furniture involve determining how the various pieces of equipment will be housed on the furniture. The CPU (central processing unit), for example, may sit on the top of the table surface or it may be housed in a special holder under the worksurface. If a CPU holder is purchased, make sure it is large enough to accommodate the size of the CPU to be used by the library, now and in the future. Also, consider how easily staff can access the entire CPU when it is in the holder, whether the library will require some kind of locking mechanism for the CPU holder, and how much air circulation will be provided to the equipment placed in the holder. A computer keyboard and mouse used on library furniture may sit directly on the worksurface, or may be housed on a pullout shelf. Space on the worksurface may also be needed for speakers or scanners.

Consider how printing will be handled. Will each computer have its own printer (so space will be needed on the worksurface), or will

FIGURE 18

Main Library renovation, Texas Tech University, Lubbock, Texas. Architects, F & S Partners and Parkhill, Smith & Cooper, Inc. Photo used by permission of the photographer. Photo credit: Robert Suddarth Photographer.

all of the printing be networked to a central printer located away from the computers? Have other furnishings been designed to hold the central printer? Where debit cards will be used, has space been planned to accommodate card dispensers and printing equipment? In situations where limited space is available, the ability of a worksurface to hold the required computer equipment can be checked by developing a scale drawing of the tabletop (from plan view—looking down on the table from above), with each piece of equipment drawn to scale or with scaled cutouts of the equipment that can be arranged on the drawing of the tabletop.

When a new building is planned, decisions regarding how computer tables will be powered should be made before the electrical plans are completed. Power can be provided from electrical outlets at each computer location. More than one duplex outlet will be needed at each location, however. Alternatively, on tables with one or two computers, power may be accessed from a power strip mounted on the underside of the worksurface. The power strip then plugs into an outlet in the floor or wall.

Another solution involves purchasing computer workstations supplied with integrated electrical systems (for example, eight-wire, three-circuit systems) that are wired to building power from a single junction box. The outlets in the system are then attached to the piece of furniture at regular intervals. The use of furniture with an integrated electrical system is recommended where computers are placed on long rows of workstations. Integrated electrical systems are useful in building renovations in order to avoid trenching concrete floors. A range of workstations can be powered easily from one point—from electricity brought through a wall or down a building column—and wired to the furniture electrical system.

In discussions with architects and electrical engineers who are not familiar with libraries, the local planning team should discuss the number of circuits that will be provided in areas with numerous computers. Explain that, because of the popularity of computers in libraries, it is possible that every computer will be in use at one time.

Most libraries still provide data for networked computers and printers by cabling through conduit to termination points for data jacks in the floor or the wall. Patch cords are then used to carry data to computers. The use of wireless data transmission has, however, made it possible to add networked computers to areas of the library where conduit has not been provided for data.

Access to power and data below the worksurface of a computer table can be accomplished by supplying grommets through the worksurface. A more flexible method is the use of a cord-drop slot, a minimum of 2" deep, located at the back of a worksurface. The slot allows cords and cables to drop at any point along the worksurface. On a computer table that is one large, flat surface with panel ends, the tabletop is constructed in two pieces in order to allow for the slot in the middle. The slot should be supplied with a retaining strip to prevent pencils or other small objects from falling through to the floor. On computer workstations that are built with back and side panels, the worksurface is recessed away from the back panel to allow for the cord drop.

The problem of wire management is the same on computer tables as it is on service desks. The mesh bag mentioned in regard to service desks works well on large computer tables. Custom-built, panel-end computer tables may be built with a "box" running along the length of the middle of the table, under the top. The box holds and hides all of the cords and cables from the computers. Lockable doors in the box provide access to hidden cords and cables.

Public-access computers are used in libraries on large, flat tables with no dividers and on rows of starter/adder carrels with low intermediate panels or with low or high dividers. Library-furniture manufacturers make all shapes and sizes of furniture for computer workstations, including six-sided or round tables that can be designed to fit around building columns. (See figure 19.) Computer tables can also be individual units designed especially for wheelchair use. Many computer tables have laminate tops with wood edge bands. Tabletops that are self-edged with laminate are not recommended, because the laminate can easily break. Where the extensive use of computers is expected, a polyvinyl chloride (PVC) edge on computer tables or carrels may be used.

Some interior designers prefer to use commercial products made by office-furniture manufacturers to hold public-access computers. Components of office-panel systems and furniture designed especially for computer classrooms or information areas (like KI's Workzone tables or Worden's Pavilion series) work well in the library because of their built-in electrical systems and wire-management capabilities.

FIGURE 19

Carroll High School, Southlake Independent School District, Southlake, Texas. Architects, SHW Group, Inc. Mezitta computer tables, Serpentine Unit, manufactured by BCI. Photo used by permission of Libra-Tech Corporation. Photo credit: Penny Schmitz.

Some libraries have opted to provide computers with recessed monitors (discussed previously for use with circulation desks). Recessed monitors provide more privacy for individual users; however, they are a hindrance when a staff member is assisting a library user and both of them must see the screen at the same time. Recessed monitors would not be workable in a situation where any type of collaborative computer use is expected or where visual control is a priority (for example, in a school library). (See figure 20.)

Computers can also be placed on built-in millwork or on architectural woodwork counters built against a wall. All of the requirements regarding kind of use by library patrons, size and amount of equipment to be housed, electrical and data access, and wire-management capabilities must be considered in designing custom-built furniture for computers. In one library where educational software for children is loaded on the hard drives of individual computers, the computer monitors and keyboards are located on a 27"-high counter. The CPUs for the computers are located in lockable cabinets with louvered doors above the counter. A shallow "box" at the back of the counter (between the counter and the cabinets) covers all of the cords running between the monitors and the CPUs.

Some school and small public libraries purchase relatively inexpensive computer furniture from office- and library-supply catalogs. The furniture is available in a wide variety of standard sizes and configurations, including individual units and four-sided or six-sided modules. Purchasing from a library-supply catalog is an easy way to acquire furniture; however, many of the products in catalogs are manufactured by a company other than the one that publishes the catalog. In fact, the manufacturer's name is often provided with the

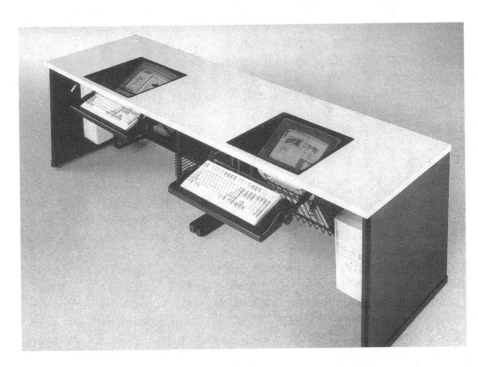

FIGURE 20

Computer table with recessed monitors. Manufactured by APW-Wright Line. Used by permission of APW-Wright Line. Photo credit: Bob Nash, Nash Photography, Worcester, Mass.

product in the catalog. In some cases, you may obtain the same product for a lower price by going directly to a dealer of the product rather than by purchasing through a catalog. Information about a manufacturer can often be obtained by locating the company's phone number on its home page on the World Wide Web. Call the company and ask for the name of a dealer or representative in your area. Then call the dealer to obtain more information about the product and to obtain the dealer's price.

Computer classrooms or labs are now considered a standard space for all types of libraries. Computer labs can be equipped with standard computer tables placed in rows in classroom style or with millwork counters built around the perimeter of the room. The disadvantage of built-in furniture arranged around the walls is that participants in a class or workshop have to turn their chairs to see the instructor. Computer classrooms may be furnished with tables for holding recessed or partially recessed monitors. Recessed monitors allow participants in training sessions to see the presenter easily when the instructor is at the front of the room; however, some trainers prefer to work at the back of the training area with information projected on a screen at the front of the room. When the presenter is at the back of the room and personal computers are placed on the tabletop, the instructor can view the screens of all hands-on participants and can see at a glance who is keeping up with the training.

Tables and Chairs

In many areas of the library, tables are a primary interior design element. In libraries where heavy use is expected, durability and performance are as important as aesthetics in selecting a table.

The American Library Association, through the staff of *Library Technology Reports*, supports an extensive program of performance-testing of library tables and chairs that began in the 1970s. Most of the work was carried out by Carl Eckelman, professor of wood science at the Forest and Natural Resources Product Laboratory at Purdue University. The data collected as the result of Eckelman's extensive performance-testing of tables provide library-furniture and other manufacturers with the information needed to engineer and design tables that will not fail with heavy use. From the performance-testing studies completed in 1977, designers know that the quality of a table depends on engineering that reflects the need for balanced construction; that is, each of the components must be as strong and as well made as any other so that the table does not fail because of one weak element.[3]

When selecting tables for libraries, consider how the top of the table will be used. In order to prevent a table from sagging, any table that is selected to hold heavy computer or microform equipment or index racks for heavy books must be built with double keels 8" to 12" deep running the length of the underside of the table. Even simple study tables longer than 60" that lack an apron to provide support along the length of the table may require some kind of V-shaped steel brace or other supporting member to keep them from sagging or deflecting in the middle. Study tables 48" wide or wider by 72" long or longer usually require one or two wood keels for support.

Tables for libraries can be designed or specified in a wide variety of sizes and shapes. (See figures 21, 22, and 23.) When selecting tables for adults, it is important to keep in mind a person's desire to maintain personal space in a public facility. A table should be large enough to allow two or more individuals to sit at it comfortably and continue to feel secure in their own space. In a library where study tables are expected to be used for research, tables should be at least 48" wide and 72" long. In a genealogy library or room, large tables are needed to allow each user to spread out a number of books that are studied together. With small tables (30" or 36" wide × 60" or 66" long), only one person, or possibly two, may feel comfortable sitting at the same table.

Library tabletops may be supported by legs or by panel ends. Tables with full panel ends are massive in appearance and are used more suitably in large spaces where the tables are not out of proportion with other furnishings, as well as with the total size of the space. Tables with Mission-style end panels are not as massive as full-panel ends and can be used in smaller spaces. Small round tables are used in libraries in children's areas, in young adult areas, or in any space where conversing or working together is encouraged.

Many tables in libraries are wired to supply power and data at tabletop or to supply power for task lights. Any table wired to supply power and data must be specified with a chase that holds separate channels for power and data running from the floor or the wall of the

FIGURE 21

Law library, Kilpatrick Stockton LLP, Atlanta, Georgia. Tables and chairs manufactured by Thos. Moser Cabinetmakers. Photo used by permission of Thos. Moser Cabinetmakers. Photo credit: Thomas Watkins, Atlanta, Ga.

building up to the tabletop. On leg-base tables, the chase is usually attached to a table leg, or the leg itself is hollowed out to serve as a chase. On panel-end tables, the chase is hidden by one of the end panels. A table should also include a wire-management channel to hide cords from the power/data box on the table; the channel runs along the underside of the length of the table, to the chase.

In coordinating furniture and building plans, electrical plans should be prepared as an overlay of the furniture plans in order to coordinate the exact location of power and data floor boxes. Electrical locations should match one corner of leg-base tables or one of the ends of the panel-end tables where the power/data chase will carry power and data to the tabletop. All library-furniture manufacturers offer some type of box with a pop-up lid for public table-top access to power and data.

The tables made by library-furniture manufacturers and those engineered for durability and made by commercial-furniture manufacturers are suitable for any library. In large library building projects, tables are often custom-designed by architects and interior designers in order to make the building's interior more distinctive and functional. Distinctive features for a smaller library project can be achieved by placing a customized design on the end panels of standard library furniture tables.

Library tables can have veneer tops or laminate-faced tops. Tables with laminate tops should have solid wood edges—tops self-edged with laminate are not durable. Veneer tabletops are usually specified for special collection rooms where use can be carefully monitored. One busy special library that opened with veneer table-

FIGURE 22

Shields Library, University of California at Davis. Chairs, tables, and carrels manufactured by Fetzers' Inc. Photo used by permission of Fetzers' Inc. Photo credit: Richard Springgate.

FIGURE 23

Library, Agnes Scott College, Atlanta/Decatur, Georgia. Furniture manufactured by Thos. Moser Cabinetmakers. Photo used by permission of Thos. Moser Cabinetmakers. Photo credit: Thomas Watkins, Atlanta, Ga.

tops added glass sheets over the veneer soon after the library opening, when it became clear that the veneer would not withstand heavy use.

While attractive tables are desirable for a library, a table is only as useful as the chair that is placed with it. Library users must be comfortable sitting in a chair for short and long periods of time. In busy school, academic, and public libraries, the durability and comfort of the reading chairs selected are as important as the look of the chairs. Effective interior design involves making decisions which ensure that library chairs will be attractive and useful for many years to come.

Like tables, the topic of chairs for libraries has been researched extensively for more than 20 years by the American Library Association, through the work of the staff of *Library Technology Reports* (*LTR*). In a report published in 1995, Howard S. White, former editor of *LTR*, said he hoped that performance-testing would "eventually lead to an American National Standard, which would expand the number and types of chairs that could be specified for library use while assuring they would not fail in the very demanding environment of libraries."[4]

White's comment is the key to selecting chairs for any library—chairs for school, public, and academic libraries must be strong enough not to fail with extensive use and abuse. It is the responsibility of design professionals and consultants to select chairs that will not fail for many years. In order to choose durable chairs for areas of the library with expected heavy use, select a chair that has been performance-tested to the *LTR* or comparable standards, or a chair that has been used in a busy library for 10 years without failure. The furniture maker Buckstaff, for example, tests to a British standard that is comparable to, or more stringent than, the *LTR* tests.

A chair that is designed specifically for a project or one that has not previously been used in a busy library should be sent to the Forest and Natural Resources Product Laboratory at Purdue University or some other independent facility to be tested to the *LTR* standards. The Dakota Jackson library chair selected for use in the main facility at the San Francisco Public Library was performance-tested twice at Purdue before it was specified. The designer altered the chair after each performance test, with the result that the final design met the stringent standards of the *LTR* tests.

The major library-furniture manufacturers in the United States have participated in the development of the *LTR* tests and are aware of the need for performance-testing. The *LTR* performance standards are more stringent than standards developed by the American National Standards Institute (ANSI) and the Business and Institutional Furniture Manufacturers Association (BIFMA). Chairs that are manufactured for commercial use—but not specifically for library use—often have passed the ANSI/BIFMA tests. Chairs made for commercial use that have passed ANSI/BIFMA standards may be durable enough for library use; however, check the durability of the chairs in previous settings with heavy use prior to purchasing them.

Chairs that have passed the ANSI/BIFMA standards may be acceptable only in areas where light use is expected.

Reading chairs to be used at tables or carrels in libraries do not have to be expensive to be durable. The same inexpensive Jasper chair that can be seen in hundreds of restaurants around the United States can be used successfully in libraries. All of the library-furniture manufacturers continue to supply standard leg- or sled-based library chairs with upholstered seats and backs. Many libraries are, however, selecting all-wood chairs rather than upholstered chairs, because of ease of maintenance. If chairs with arms are to be used at reading tables, make sure that the arms will fit under the tables and that library users won't smash their fingers if they pull the chair close to the table.

Instead of all-wood chairs, interior designers may select a chair with a wood seat and back and a steel frame and legs, an all-metal chair, or an upholstered chair with a steel frame. Regardless of the chair selected, its durability should be documented either by performance-testing data or by heavy use over a long period of time in a library or similar setting.

Because of the length of time now spent by library users at computers, an armless task chair with pneumatic height adjustment and built-in lumbar support is recommended at seated-height computers. Dozens of companies make task chairs available in a wide range of costs. Task chairs that have been performance-tested should be used, unless the library is prepared to replace the chairs every three to five years. The purchase of task chairs from an office-supply catalog is not recommended, unless the vendor can obtain performance-testing data for the chairs. All of the major office-furniture companies (such as Herman Miller, Knoll, and Steelcase) manufacture performance-tested task chairs with long-term warranties. The chair may cost more at the time of purchase, but will cost less per year with long-term service.

Most libraries have some type of soft or lounge seating in addition to reading chairs at tables and carrels. In many libraries, for example, those in large urban facilities, maintenance and durability are the most important factors in selecting lounge seating. In some public libraries, single lounge chairs, rather than two- or three-place sofas, are placed in some areas to discourage people who want to lie down to sleep in the library. On the other hand, in academic libraries where students may spend most of the night in the library, lounge seating may be provided with the intent of allowing students a chance to nap between study sessions.

Commercial, rather than residential, lounge furniture should be used in any library. The same concern about durability that applies to reader's chairs applies to lounge seating. Lounge seating expected to have heavy use in a library should meet stringent GSA Specification FNAE-80-214 or equivalent performance-testing standards. Lounge seating with wood arms or wood arm caps requires less frequent reupholstering or cleaning than chairs with fully upholstered arms. In selecting lounge furniture, discuss with vendors how easily particular pieces can be reupholstered. Where maintenance is an issue, avoid chairs that have crevices where dirt can collect.

Many commercial-furniture manufacturers, as well as library-furniture manufacturers, sell lounge seating. Lounge seating with a designer label, made from the best materials and covered with leather, may be very expensive. On the other hand, a wide variety of attractive lounge chairs and sofas is available for a reasonable price. The cost of lounge furniture can depend on the design, the cost of the materials and durability of the frame, and the type of upholstery used. Lounge seating can be upholstered in a wide range of fabrics, leather, and vinyl. Vinyl upholstery that has the softness and appearance of leather is available.

In a public library where people of all ages use lounge seating, it is important to select a chair or sofa that anyone can sit down on and get up from easily. The chair needs to be proportioned for ease of use. It is disconcerting for people with short legs to sit down on a lounge chair that is so deep from front to back that it is necessary for them to perch on the edge of the seat in order to have their feet touch the floor. Older people need a chair with a firm cushion that keeps them from sinking so far into the chair that it is difficult to get up on their feet after sitting in it.

Benches are used in libraries as casual seating in waiting and browsing areas. Benches are available from many library- and commercial-furniture manufacturers as standard items, or they may be custom-designed on special projects. Standard benches may be supported by a sled base or by panel ends. A simple wood bench may have a wood or an upholstered seat. Larger benches are available with wood frames that include backs and arms. These benches may have wood seats or an upholstered seat pad. All-metal benches, or benches with a steel frame and an upholstered seat pad, are also available.

Sled-base or leg-base backless stools are used in special situations. Stools can be used at computer workstations that are meant for a quick reference to the catalog or other resources. Stools are also frequently used as seating at computers in children's areas.

Chairs designed specifically for children come and go on the market relatively frequently, because of the small quantities purchased relative to other furniture items. All of the major library-furniture manufacturers offer chairs for children. Some of the chairs are of similar design to a line of chairs for adults offered by the same manufacturer. A good children's chair is not an adult chair with the legs cut off; the entire chair should be proportioned, with shorter legs and smaller members. The height of the chair needed will depend on the age of the children expected to use it and the height of the table with which it will be used. Chairs with a seat height of 12" to 14" should be used with tables 20" to 22" high. Chairs with a seat height of 15" to 16" should be used with tables 24" to 26" high.

Chairs selected for a particular use should be in proportion to the other furnishings around them. If a library has a simple leg-based table for reading, for example, a large, plush, upholstered reading chair with arms might not be in proportion to the table.

It is very important to try out reader's chairs (and sometimes lounge chairs) before they are purchased. In some cases, library staff or board members may visit the booths of library-furniture manufacturers and sit on chairs that are available there. In any case, vendors expect to provide sample chairs for a design team to try out before a selection is made for purchase. No charge is made to a potential customer for borrowing a chair, but the chair should be returned to the vendor after it has been tried out, unless arrangements are made to buy the sample chair as part of the purchase process.

It is not uncommon for a professional design team or the local planning team to request chairs from several vendors to try out at their office or at the library for several days. Library staff and users are sometimes asked to sit in the chairs and comment on their comfort. It is important that the same chair be comfortable for a person of small stature as well as for a person of large stature. For example, the Harold Washington chair (designed for the Harold Washington Library Center in Chicago) manufactured by the F. W. Lombard Company has been tried out and found comfortable by a number of planning teams in various parts of the country.

In bidding situations, several similar chairs made by different manufacturers may be specified as approved items. Many manufacturers offer a simple wooden chair with a wooden seat and a slat back. In order to obtain the best price, the library may be willing to purchase any one of the several chairs that meet general specifications.

Millwork and Architectural Woodwork

Most of the furnishings in a library are purchased as separate items that are not attached to the building. Some items, designated as "casework" or "millwork," are built into the library space and are constructed as part of the building contract. Millwork consists of custom-fabricated components built with lumber. Millwork includes cabinetry, paneling, custom doors and frames, furniture, and special interior trim. Millwork items should be shown in detail in the library blueprints by the architect and should be reviewed by the planning team to ensure that the millwork is functional. Some of the items often provided as millwork in libraries include counter and overhead cabinets in work areas, shelves in offices, and special storage areas. Millwork is also used in public areas for computer workstations and service desks.

Architects who are familiar with designing cabinets and counters for other types of structures may not understand the needs of a library. For example, in library work areas, counters that will be used with computers should be a minimum of 30" deep. Cabinets placed above counters must be high enough above the countertop to allow for a personal computer to be used below wall-attached cabinets. Library staff should inform the design team of any work counters that should be standing height (36" to 39") rather than seated height (29"). Seated-height counters must be built without an apron under the top, so that staff using the counter will have plenty of space to get their knees under the counter.

In children's work areas, staff may request large millwork drawers or shelves for storing large pieces of paper and special millwork bins for housing theme boxes. Staff should be asked to supply the dimensions for the items to be stored.

Computer counters for children and adults can be built as millwork. In designing the casework, the architect and interior designer must work closely with the staff to determine functional dimensions and discuss the use to be made of the millwork. The location of power and data outlets, wire management, and access to CPUs (in situations where they are housed in cabinets) should be determined in consultation with the library staff.

Millwork in the work areas of a library is often completely faced with laminate. In public areas, however, millwork may be finished in wood veneer to match other furniture pieces. In some library areas, such as special collection rooms, casework may be built by an architectural woodworking company with expertise in fine woodworking. Architectural woodworking may be used for the cabinetry where special collections of books and memorabilia are housed and on entrances and walls designed to be showplaces in a library. As noted previously, in selecting wood shelving, consideration should be given to the fact that the wood may put library materials at risk.

Planning and Furnishing Work Areas

In order to provide workable and comfortable spaces for staff, design professionals should conduct a workplace audit by interviewing library administrators, supervisors, and individual staff members. If a new library is planned, designers should observe how staff members are working in their current spaces. Unfortunately, an existing building situation is sometimes so poor that staff members find it difficult to tell planners what they would like to have in a new library, and design professionals can gain little knowledge of how a new building should function from looking at the current facility.

While it is necessary to confer with current staff in designing work spaces, it is the responsibility of the architect and interior designer to provide an objective perspective on planning work areas. It is sometimes necessary to point out flexible options to staff who want to design a space of their very own that may not be adaptable to the needs of future staff using the same space. Sometimes staff, including a library director, have to be reminded that this new building will not be theirs forever.

In small libraries, all the behind-the-scenes work may be done in a single workroom that is furnished with desks, paneled workstations, and tables or counters for staff and volunteers. In one carefully designed space, staff may handle library circulation and reference services; materials selection; the acquisition, cataloging, and processing of new materials; outreach services; library accounting; and programming activities for adults and children. In very small libraries, the workroom may be the home of the CPU and other equipment that run the library's automation system. In addition, workroom space must include storage areas for office supplies, small audiovisual equipment, and programming materials.

Larger libraries may contain all or some of the staff spaces listed here. A brief explanation of some of the work that occurs in each area is also provided.

Behind-the-scenes circulation work spaces. Books and other materials are checked in when they are returned, materials are sorted and put on carts to be returned to the shelves, and other circulation-related activities occur.

Reference work areas. Staff review newly received reference books, work at individual computer stations studying how to use new Internet sites and electronic databases, read reviews of books and other new materials for purchase, and prepare bibliographies and other teaching materials.

Collection-development work areas. In large public libraries, staff responsible for coordinating materials selection for the library system study reviews in periodicals and consider sample materials in preparation for ordering items for the library collections. (In large academic libraries, subject specialists responsible for developing various areas of the collection have individual offices.)

Technical-services work areas. Staff purchase materials to be added to the collections; check-in, catalog, and process materials for the collections; and maintain the library's cataloging records.

Work areas for school libraries and children's areas in public libraries. Staff prepare programs for children's activities, read reviews of books and other materials for purchase, and prepare special displays for children.

Technology work areas. Staff manage and maintain the library's network and automation system; repair hardware; load software on computers; generate computer reports; and work with other library departments, such as cataloging and circulation.

Outreach areas. In public libraries, staff select and store library collections and programming materials for mobile library services to day-care centers, nutrition sites, senior centers, retirement homes, and homebound individuals.

Receiving and delivery areas. Staff working in receiving and delivery provide support for the technical-services, outreach, technology, and other departments whose work is closely tied to materials and equipment coming into or going out of the library. In libraries with multiple outlets, staff in receiving and delivery sort and dispatch the delivery of items from one library to another within the library system.

Administrative spaces. Offices are provided for the library director and assistant or associate directors, as well as other administrative personnel, such as the receptionist, secretaries, business officer, and human resources officer. Administrative areas may also include work areas for copying and file storage, conference rooms or boardrooms, and coffee bars.

Public information offices. Staff responsible for publicizing and promoting the library prepare press releases for library events and regular activities; prepare and print library publications such as monthly calendars, flyers, and signs announcing special events; and prepare displays for the library.

Other staff areas. These may include preservation and archives, media production, and maintenance and custodial areas.

The kinds of furnishings selected for library work areas are related to the management philosophy of the library administration. Libraries that work in teams on a daily basis need more flexibility in the arrangement of the space and in the types of furnishings used than libraries where individuals work on assigned tasks alone. In some libraries, staff members change teams depending on the project or assignment on which they are working at any one time. In this kind of situation, each staff member may have an assigned "home base" in a cubicle or at a desk and may move to a conference area to work with other members of a team. Where team management is extremely flexible, staff members may have their home base moved as a team assignment is changed. In order to provide functional work areas and furnishings, architects, interior designers, and consultants must study the manner in which a particular staff operates in designing that staff's space. However, it is always necessary to keep in mind that the management philosophy may change in the future. Flexibility is the key to designing work areas that will be functional now and for many years to come.

Office-panel systems are touted as providing flexible work area arrangements; however, in libraries where an experienced maintenance staff is not available to reconfigure the panels, these systems cannot be changed easily. Also, unless power and data are provided in a work area with a raised floor or with a tight grid of conduit (for example, power and data every five feet), office configurations cannot be moved because power and data are not accessible. Nothing beats the flexibility of a freestanding desk that can be moved easily. Office-furniture manufacturers offer furniture systems with freestanding components and attached panels that mimic traditional office-panel systems. Many commercial manufacturers have responded to the concept of team management by providing movable conferencing units.

Planning for work areas should involve discussing storage needs with the staff. The staff working in an existing building need to check plans for a new or renovated building in order to ensure that everything useful in the old building will have a space in the new building. Storage areas requiring shelving should be equipped with strong, four-post, industrial steel shelving of an adequate depth, rather than plywood shelves hung on pegs or K-V track.

In planning a new library, design professionals should make sure that every staff member and volunteer has a place to store a coat and other outer gear and a secure place, such as a locker, for personal belongings. Also, work areas in large libraries may include coffee bars for staff and conference rooms or areas for staff meetings. Library staff should be asked by design professionals whether they prefer one large conference table or several smaller tables that can be pushed together to form a larger conference table. Sometimes folding tables or special mobile activity tables are used for meetings in order to allow for moving some of the tables out of the conference area for use elsewhere.

The type of furnishings to be used for managers' offices in a library should be discussed with the library staff and the local planning team. Traditionally, a library director's office is furnished with wood furniture, while other managers' offices may be furnished with steel office furniture with laminate or wood-veneer tops.

In public libraries, apparent opulence in staff offices can be a public relations nightmare if local residents believe that more of the project budget should have been spent on furnishing the public areas of a new building. In some situations, local planning teams believe that old pre-computer furniture can be used in a new building. In such cases, it is the job of the design professionals to point out that the old furniture is no longer functional and that the library needs desks or workstations that are the ergonomically correct height and depth for computer work, with worksurfaces large enough to allow staff to work efficiently.

Circulation Workrooms

These usually include closed offices for one or more circulation managers and open workstations, desks, or counters for other staff. One area of the circulation work space will be used for checking in materials returned at outdoor or indoor book drops and at the circulation desk. In some libraries, books and other materials drop directly into the circulation work area or a sorting room through strategically placed return chutes outside the building or inside, near the circulation desk. The type of computer and security equipment needed by the library for check-in will determine the type of furnishings and the layout of the return area. In order to design a functional area, the architect or designer should work directly with staff to determine the requirements for furniture and adjacencies in the materials-return area.

Close to check-in space, staff will place returned materials on steel library shelving. The returned materials on the shelves will be sorted by call number and placed on book trucks prior to being reshelved in public areas. Close to sorting shelves, floor space should be left open for storing book trucks. Design professionals should discuss the volume of circulation expected in order to determine how many sorting shelves and book trucks should be planned for a new or renovated building. (Keep in mind that, in a public library, circulation may increase greatly with a move into a new building.)

Depending on how large a library is and how it operates, a circulation work area may include space for checking the condition of returned audiovisual materials, preparing overdue notices, handling books put on hold or reserve by library users, and other circulation-related tasks. (Large libraries with substantial budgets may want to install one of the sophisticated computerized book-moving devices now available.)

Reference and Collection-Development Work Areas

These may be furnished with individual desks in shared space, desks in individual offices, or office-panel system cubicles. Shelves for holding new reference materials, professional book collections, and materials to be reviewed are provided in the work areas. A conference table for staff meetings may be part of an open area or may be in a separate conference room. Individual offices are usually provided for one or more managers of reference services or collection development. In large academic libraries, subject specialists responsible for collection development each have their own separate office.

Technical-Services Work Areas

These should be designed to reflect the flow of materials into the building and out to the shelves. The interior designer should work with the staff to develop a formal or informal flow chart that illustrates how materials move through the department.

Staff members in charge of the acquisitions function for the library order most materials online from companies that sell books and audiovisual materials to libraries and bookstores. When materials are received, they are checked in by a receiving clerk or by the acquisitions department. Usually, new materials will be moved next to the cataloging department. After cataloging has been completed, materials will be moved to the processing department, where property stamps and labels are placed on the items and, in some cases, plastic covers are placed on books.

The design of each technical-services workstation should be based on supporting the work to be done at that particular location.

For example, it is necessary for the interior designer to know the kinds of tasks to be performed at each workstation, the kinds and maximum amounts of materials to be stored, the kinds of equipment to be used, the power and data requirements, and any special furnishings to be used adjacent to the workstation.

Either individual desks or paneled workstations can be used in technical-services departments; however, some staff may prefer the privacy of a cubicle in order to have fewer distractions and less noise. Every desk or workstation in the technical-services area must have empty space next to it for one or more book trucks to hold work in process. Worksurfaces must be large enough to accommodate a computer with plenty of space around it for spreading out piles of books and other materials. Either an L- or U-shaped work space with more than one worksurface is preferred. All worksurfaces should be 30" deep and 29" high. Overhead shelves are convenient for holding manuals and other work materials.

The processing of materials may be done at large tables or deep counters, rather than at desks. Libraries that do a lot of their own processing (rather than buying materials preprocessed) sometimes have special storage requirements related to the processing worksurface. In some cases, a millwork counter built with shelves for plastic book covers and other supplies may be preferred by the library staff.

Work Areas for School Libraries and Children's Areas in Public Libraries

These are unique because of the kinds of programming activities offered to young people. In addition to offices for managers and individual desks for other staff and volunteers, work areas must include large tables or counter areas for preparing programming materials. Often tabletop or countertop space is needed for a laminating machine or a die-cut machine, such as an Ellison machine.

Children's staff require special storage areas not used by any other group of library employees. Ready-made flat files or horizontal millwork shelves large enough to hold poster paper are needed. Millwork should also be built to provide vertical spaces for holding large props and board books upright in slots 36" or higher.

Many children's librarians store dozens of bankers boxes or other cartons referred to as "theme" boxes. Each box contains the props and materials needed to present a program on a particular topic to toddlers, preschoolers, and school-age children. Library staff should provide information about the size and number of boxes required to the architect. The boxes are usually stored on millwork shelves built to the specifications of the library or on steel four-post shelving.

Children's librarians may require special puppet "trees" or other hanging devices for puppets, as well as storage space for portable puppet theatres. Children's librarians also keep paper, craft supplies, scissors, costumes, and a wide variety of unusual objects that are used for young people's programs. All of these materials require storage in a closet supplied with open floor space, shelves, and hanging rods. In school libraries, a large storage area may be needed once or twice a year for a large number of boxes of books to be sold in a book fair. In public libraries, space may be needed to store a number of boxes of summer reading club material sent to the local library by the state library. (These storage spaces may not necessarily be in the children's area, but the architect and interior designer should know that empty storage space for these items should be included somewhere in the building.)

Technology Work Areas

These should be located adjacent to the computer room that houses the library's servers and its local area network (LAN) and wide area network (WAN) management systems. Desks or paneled workstations used by technology staff should be earth-grounded. The grounding provides static control when staff are working on the inside of computers with the cases removed. The planning team may desire separate paneled cubicles for each staff member in order to provide a quiet area for focusing on hardware and software problems. Technology staff may also require large tables or workbench areas for handling repairs and loading software. Storage for cables and other small peripherals should be located in cabinets or drawers close to the work areas. The technology department may require a large storage room or open space for housing new equipment not yet installed, old computers not yet removed from inventory, equipment boxes used for transporting computers, and equipment held in reserve.

The computer room itself will accommodate much of the equipment on racks; however, network servers can be housed on special LAN-management furniture, such as the system manufactured by APW-Wright Line. (See figure 24.) Computer equipment should be located in a secured area with temperature and humidity that are controlled to relate to the size of the area and the number of servers housed in the room. In order to have a dust-free environment, the computer room should have a hard-surface floor rather than carpet. The room should be located close to the power and communication feeds into the building. (The computer room and the phone closet should be two separate spaces.) Ideally, the computer room should have raised flooring to provide easy access to data and power when more equipment is added or when equipment is moved to a new location in the room.

Receiving and Delivery Areas

These are needed in even the smallest libraries. In small libraries, the receiving area should include a standing-height workbench for sorting mail and mail slots for each staff member. Sometimes interlibrary loan materials are prepared for shipping at the receiving counter. In this case, mailing supplies, a mail scale, and a postage meter may be located at the receiving counter.

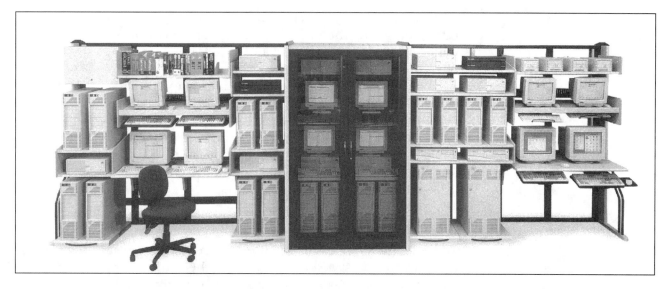

FIGURE 24

LAN-management furniture system. Manufactured by APW-Wright Line. Used by permission of APW-Wright Line. Photo credit: Bob Nash, Nash Photography, Worcester, Mass.

In large libraries with multiple outlets, the sorting of items going from branch to branch is usually done near the receiving area of the main library. The receiving area is equipped with large commercial steel shelves or bins to hold smaller bags or bins of returned library materials, new books and audiovisual items, office supplies, and interoffice mail moving from one library to another. The interior designer or consultant should discuss the size and number of bins and boxes that the library staff expects to store temporarily in the sorting area. Some libraries prefer to have large industrial tables for sorting in the receiving area.

In a large library system where office and other supplies are purchased centrally and sent out to branches as they are requested, the central supply area should be located close to the receiving area. Similarly, the arrangement of the library should allow new items coming from the technical-services area after cataloging and processing to move easily to the sorting area to be distributed to the various libraries. Because all items moving into and out of the building are stored temporarily in the receiving area, the space must be large enough to accommodate pallets of boxes, book trucks, furniture items to be delivered to other buildings, and a variety of other items that come in through the loading dock.

In public libraries, the receiving area often becomes the temporary home of large numbers of boxes of donated books. The receipt of these books is a mixed blessing for most libraries. In planning a new building, the architect should assist the library staff in designing space for donated books. Usually, the books are actually donated to the Friends of the Library organization, which subsequently sells the books, with the proceeds from the sale going to the library. Most Friends groups do not have space outside the library, so the library must provide a storage area for the book donations and must also provide space for members of the Friends to sort the books in preparation for selling them. The handling of donated books sounds like a minor matter to an outsider, but to the library staff, space for handling donations is essential.

In some libraries, the space for storing and sorting books may be close to the receiving area. In other libraries, staff request that the Friends area be close to the library entrance so that the room can be open to the public at designated times for special book sales. In either case, the book-donation area needs plenty of shelving (maybe from the old library), empty floor space for piling boxes of books, and large tables for sorting books.

Administrative Spaces

These include offices for the library director and associate or assistant directors, as well as offices for other administrative personnel such as the business officer and human resources director. In some libraries, offices may also be provided for other staff, for example, library development and fundraising managers, staff-training personnel, and a coordinator of volunteers.

A basic fact in planning administrative spaces is that the director and other library officials want offices with windows. In small libraries, the director's office may have the same type of furnishings used in other work areas. In larger libraries, the director may have an office that is part of a group of spaces that include a private rest room, a boardroom or conference room, a separate work space that visitors do not see, a secretary or administrative assistant's work area, and a coffee bar. Many directors prefer an office that includes a large desk and appropriately handsome chair, a credenza or other storage area, a computer workstation (if one is not incorporated into the desk), a small conference table with four to six guest chairs, bookshelves, and sometimes an informal seating area with a small sofa and coffee table. Filing cabinets may be located in the office or in a nearby work area. An office with all of these items may seem ostentatious; however, it is important to keep in mind that the director is the person most responsible in the organization for meeting with the officials of the library's funding body. The image that the director projects to officials, contributors, and policy-makers is important for the entire library.

NOTES

1. Ann Massman, "The Wood Shelving Dilemma," *Library Resources and Technical Services* 44, no. 4 (October 2000): 209–13.

2. For detailed descriptions of wood and steel shelving systems, see Carol R. Brown, *Planning Library Interiors: The Selection of Furnishings for the Twenty-First Century* (Phoenix: Oryx, 1995), 34–43.

3. For a discussion of the performance-testing of tables, see Brown, *Planning Library Interiors*, 73.

4. Carl A. Eckelman, "Library Chairs: An Overview of the Library Technology Reports Test Method with Test Reports on 30 Chairs," *Library Technology Reports* (March–April 1995).

Signs and Wayfinding

In a successfully planned library interior, all the design elements work together in harmony to provide a functional, convenient, and attractive building. If any one feature of the library is ignored in planning an integrated design, the overall success of the library will suffer. Unfortunately, one area that is sometimes ignored or left out of the budget in small library projects is a sign system. The result is the tacking-on of homemade or uncoordinated signs that detract from other successfully designed elements of a new or renovated library interior.

In large projects, the sign system for a new or renovated building should be planned by a sign consultant hired specifically for the job or by the interior designer, architect, or consultant. In small projects, the library staff can plan the sign system. The design of the sign system involves consideration of both functional and aesthetic aspects. Signs should accomplish their purpose in making the facility convenient for library users, and should enhance rather than detract from the "overall visual experience" as quoted from John Pile in the first chapter.

In large projects, an architect, interior designer, or sign consultant designs and specifies all aspects of the system, including the shape, size, and type of lettering; fabrication; finish; and materials. (See figure 25.) The signs are manufactured by a company specializing in the fabrication of signs. In projects where bidding is required, the fabrication of the signs is bid according to the specifications developed by the design professionals.

In smaller projects, the architect, interior designer, consultant, or staff may select standard sign products from a vendor, such as ASI's Interior 20 PaperFlex system. Small libraries may also purchase signs from a library-supply catalog. Some sign vendors offer standard products and also use their standard materials to fabricate custom signs.

When planning a sign system, consideration must be given to the following functional types of signs:

Orientational signs enable users to orient themselves within the library and identify how to get to various areas within the building, such as the reference area, children's area, and adult bookstacks. Orientational signs include, for example, directory boards and mounted floor plans.

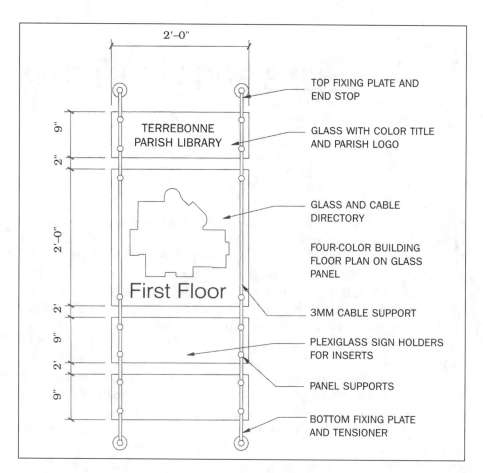

2'-0"

9"
2"
2'-0"
2'
9"
2'
9"

TERREBONNE
PARISH LIBRARY

First Floor

TOP FIXING PLATE AND
END STOP

GLASS WITH COLOR TITLE
AND PARISH LOGO

GLASS AND CABLE
DIRECTORY

FOUR-COLOR BUILDING
FLOOR PLAN ON GLASS
PANEL

3MM CABLE SUPPORT

PLEXIGLASS SIGN HOLDERS
FOR INSERTS

PANEL SUPPORTS

BOTTOM FIXING PLATE
AND TENSIONER

FIGURE 25

Drawing of lobby directory for Main Library, Terrebonne Parish, Houma, Louisiana. Sign designed by Phillips Swager Associates, architects. Used by permission of Phillips Swager Associates.

Directional signs guide users to particular locations or services within the building. Signs with arrows pointing to a particular location, for example, are directional signs.

Identification signs identify or label particular destinations or features. They include, for example, signs on the end panels of bookstacks; signs that identify particular rooms or service areas, such as rest rooms, auditorium, or information desk; donor signs; and signs that identify particular collections, such as genealogy, adult fiction, and periodicals.

Instructional signs provide instructions; for example, on how to operate a piece of equipment, such as a copier.

Regulatory signs provide library users with information on regulations or required procedures, and warn users about emergency procedures; for example, no smoking, no eating or drinking in this area, and use of pencils required in the genealogy room.

Informational or current-awareness signs provide information needed by library users, such as hours, announcements of special programs, library services offered, and out-of-order signs for equipment.

PLATE 1A

Atrium, Main Library, San Francisco Public Library. Architects, Pei Cobb Freed & Partners and Simon, Martin-Vegue, Winkelstein, Moris (SMWM). Used by permission of SMWM. Photo credit: SMWM.

PLATE 1B

Main Library, San Francisco Public Library. Design of door to special collection room reflects the design of the atrium shown above. Architects, Pei Cobb Freed & Partners and Simon, Martin-Vegue, Winkelstein, Moris. Used by permission of SMWM. Photo credit: SMWM.

PLATE 2A

Scott County Public Library, Georgetown, Kentucky. Johnson Romanowitz Architects, Charles L. Witt, principal. Furniture manufactured by the Worden Company. Photo used by permission of the photographer. Photo credit: Copyright Walt Roycraft Photography.

PLATE 2B

Davis Library, Plano, Texas. Architects, Phillips Swager Associates. Used by permission of the photographer. Photo credit: Copyright King Graf 2001.

PLATE 3A

Cleveland Public Library, Cleveland, Ohio. Architects, Hardy Holzman Pfeiffer Associates.
Used by permission of the photographer. Photo credit: Cervin Robinson.

PLATE 3B

Scott County Public Library, Georgetown, Kentucky. Johnson Romanowitz Architects, Charles
L. Witt, principal. Furniture manufactured by the Worden Company. Photo used
by permission of the photographer. Photo credit: Copyright Walt Roycraft Photography.

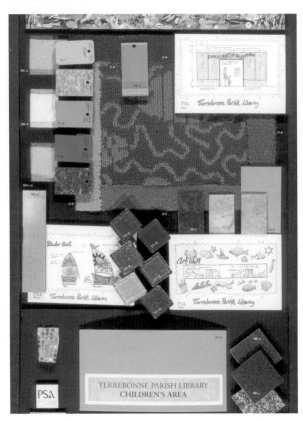

PLATE 4

Color boards for Main Library, Terrebonne Parish, Houma, Louisiana. Prepared by Phillips Swager Associates, architects. Used by permission of Phillips Swager Associates.

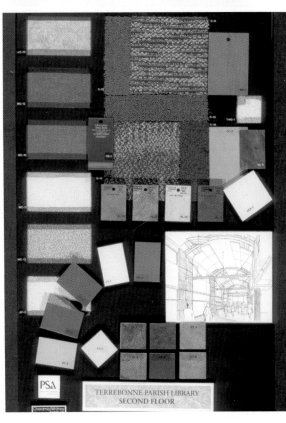

PLATE 5A

Carmel Clay Public Library, Carmel, Indiana. Terrazzo floor at main entrance. Architects,
Meyer, Scherer & Rockcastle, Ltd. Used by permission of the
photographer. Photo credit: Copyright William N. Taylor/Taylor Photo.com.

PLATE 5B

Children's area, Carmel Clay Public Library, Carmel, Indiana. Architects, Meyer,
Scherer & Rockcastle, Ltd. Used by permission of the photographer. Photo credit:
Copyright William N. Taylor/Taylor Photo.com.

PLATE 6A

Entrance to the children's area, Carrollton Public Library at Hebron and Josey,
Carrollton, Texas. Architects, F & S Partners. Used by permission of the photographer.
Photo credit: Craig Blackmon, BlackInk Architectural Photography.

PLATE 6B

Children's area, Lancaster Veterans Memorial Library, Lancaster, Texas. Architects,
Phillips Swager Associates. Used by permission of the photographer. Photo credit: On the
Mark, copyright Mark Olsen.

PLATE 7

Kentucky Room, Scott County Public Library, Georgetown, Kentucky. Johnson Romanowitz Architects, Charles L. Witt, principal. Furniture manufactured by the Worden Company. Photo used by permission of the photographer. Photo credit: Copyright Walt Roycraft Photography.

PLATE 8

Atrium, Central Library, Los Angeles Public Library. Architects, Hardy Holzman Pfeiffer Associates. Used by permission of Hardy Holzman Pfeiffer Associates. Photo credit: Foaad Farah/Hardy Holzman Pfeiffer Associates.

The planning of a sign system for a new library involves identifying and making a list of the types of signs that will be needed and deciding where these signs should be located. The task of making that determination can be accomplished by taking a virtual tour of the library using a computer model, or by simply "walking" through the building by looking at a blueprint. The goal of this is to anticipate what signs a user will need to become oriented to the general layout of the building; to find particular services, areas, and rooms; and to receive the instructions and information needed for a satisfactory library experience.

In an existing library, new signage may be planned as a special project initiated to improve the appearance and use of the building. The project should begin with an assessment or audit of existing signs. A list of signs and their locations in the building is developed. Photographs of signs and their surroundings can be taken to support the list. Pictures of existing signs are helpful in determining where an overabundance of signs exists in one place, where signs are inconsistent, and where they are unattractive. Photos also serve as useful reference devices when staff members are discussing the results of the sign audit. The list of existing signs and photographs is studied to determine which signs should be eliminated, which signs should be replaced, and what additional signs may be needed. Recommendations for future signage can be compiled using the audit information.

The following are some examples from an actual public-library sign audit accompanied by recommendations for improvements:

Identification of collections or parts of collections

"Basic skills for Self-Help"—handmade, attached to end panel.

> Replace with sign consistent with other end-panel signage.

"Adult paperback nonfiction"—computer-generated, mounted on top of book racks and on end panels.

> Replace with sign consistent with other end-panel signage.

"Biographies"—individual letters of various colors mounted vertically to a column and missing the "s."

> Where are the biographies in relation to this sign? Will an end-panel sign be sufficient?

"Fiction paperbacks"—signs mounted on top of revolving racks to indicate content.

> Leave these as they are. Consider in relation to other changes made.

"Periodicals, back issues"—mounted back in a corner on the wall—not easily seen.

> Is this necessary?

"Catalogs"—the only signs are on the computers themselves.

> Consider the impact of a hanging sign.

"How to find a book"

Information mounted on a dark board and laminated. Placed on the end panels of stacks in several areas of the building.

> Do people really read this? Is it accurate? Is it better for users to ask a librarian than read this? If you must have it, replace it with a changeable sign holder like those to be used by the typewriters.

Three instructional and informational signs by copier

Three different signs placed on the column by the copier—one sign is white with a red border, one is yellow, and one is white.

> Can these three signs be replaced by one sign in a changeable sign holder?

"No bicycles; no skateboarding" at main entrance

Computer-generated sign taped to the glass.

> Make these instructions consistent with hours posted on the glass.

"No food, drinks, etc."

Orange letters attached to the vinyl wall covering in the foyer.

> Consider how to display these regulations in relation to the directory board.

"Quiet please, please be considerate . . ."

Mounted at several locations around the library.

> Are these really necessary?

Announcement of children's and other programs

Taped to glass at the main entrance and on glass on the inside set of doors. Also, an announcement taped to a computer shield at the circulation desk.

> Purchase a directory/announcement board that allows for posting info about special events. Users will soon learn to look there for news.

Fines, number of videos and nonfiction books that can be borrowed, borrowing period, etc.

Variety of signs providing information about borrowing attached to wall behind circulation desk. Signs are white, pink, blue, and yellow with black lettering. One has a red border.

> Consider which of these signs is really necessary. Do people really read these signs, or do staff end up telling most people anyway and pointing to the sign? Can all of

these regulations be handed to new users on some kind of bookmark or flyer so the signs aren't needed? For those that are needed, replace the numerous signs with one large changeable sign to hold all of the regulations.

"Vertical file may be checked out"
Computer-generated sign mounted on top of vertical file. Undoubtedly means "vertical file material may be checked out."

Replace with a changeable sign holder consistent with others.

Based on the information collected during the sign audit and the accompanying recommendations, the library staff can work alone, with a consultant, or with a vendor to develop a sign system (as discussed below) and to purchase and install signs.

In academic and special libraries, a sign system sanctioned by the parent institution or organization may determine the details of the system to be used in the library. In new or renovated libraries without a sign policy and a carefully designed system, plans for new signs should be designed in close consultation with the library staff and with other project team members. The essential word here is "system." Signs used initially in the library should be part of a coordinated system with detailed specifications that can be replicated as the library needs replacement or additional signs in the future. The system should be easily understandable and flexible enough that, after the construction project is finished, library or institutional staff will be able to maintain the consistency of the system over time.

Consistency in signage throughout a building allows users to learn the system quickly and easily. Signs of the same type (directional, instructional, etc.) throughout a building should have the same shape, size, layout, type style, and placement, if possible. The sign system should be logical and should be given in a progression from the general to the specific. Signs should avoid the use of library jargon, such as "Bibliographic Information Center." Words should be as descriptive as possible and easily recognizable by library users. Terminology should be used consistently—only one term should be applied to any one area, service, etc.

The signs in libraries, as in all public buildings, must comply with the Americans with Disabilities Act of 1990 and any other applicable state or local regulations. The *ADA Accessibility Guidelines for Buildings and Facilities* require that all signs have a width-to-height ratio between 3:5 and 1:1 for letters and numbers. Letters and numbers are required to have a stroke width-to-height ratio between 1:5 and 1:10. Signs placed overhead must be placed a minimum of 89" above the floor and must have letters and numbers at least 3" high. Permanent signs for rooms and spaces that are installed on a wall next to a door must be mounted on the latch side of the door, 60" above the floor to the center line of the signs. Letters and numbers on permanent signs must be at least 5/8" and no more than 2" high, must be raised 1/32", and must be accompanied by Grade 2 Braille. If pictograms are used for permanent signs, the verbal equivalent must be placed directly below the symbol. The characters must contrast in color with the background. Signs should have light-colored characters on a dark background or dark-colored characters on a light background. In addition to compliance with the ADA, the details of sign systems may be controlled by local or other building codes. The Uniform Building Code, for example, has requirements for exits, stairway and door identification, room capacities, and accessibility.

A sign system should complement the architecture and the rest of the interior design of a library. The same elements of good design that apply to planning each feature of a building should be considered when designing the sign system. The dimensions of signs should be in proportion to the scale of the building and, if they are mounted on furnishings, in proportion to the scale of the furnishings. The colors and materials of the signs should coordinate with the colors and materials used throughout the building. Throughout the library, signs should be mounted and positioned in a consistent manner in relation to other building elements, so that users know where to look to obtain information. (See figure 26.)

Signs can be ceiling-hung, wall-mounted, mounted on a column, or freestanding. Freestanding signs may be large signs mounted on a metal stand or small signs designed to sit on a desk or countertop. An architect, designer, or consultant who designs the sign system will decide how signs should be mounted. In small projects where library staff plan the signs, a sign vendor will assist in determining how and where signs should be mounted. The signs used in a library may include the following:

FIGURE 26

Council Bluffs Public Library, Council Bluffs, Iowa. Leo Daly Architects. Circulation services sign manufactured by ASI Sign Systems, Grinnell, Iowa. Used by permission of Jim Godsey, Council Bluffs Public Library. Photo credit: Paul Brokering.

Building plaques that list the names of elected or institutional officials and provide other details about the construction of the building

Directory boards or maps showing the location of various departments; in a multistory library, floor locations

Boards or signs that announce library policies, special services, or events occurring in the library

Signs that indicate the location of service points—check-out and check-in desks, reserve desks, information desks, etc.

Signs that indicate the location of major functional areas—periodicals, youth department, adult nonfiction, special collections

Signs that indicate collections within a larger area, usually used in public libraries—mysteries, science fiction, picture and easy books, etc.

ADA-required room-identification signs

Signs with arrows that indicate the location of areas or services that are not visible from a main corridor

Signs at stairways or elevators that indicate that a specific area or service is located on another floor

End-panel signs on bookstacks that indicate the contents of a range. (These must be designed to allow for changing the content of the signs easily and quickly.)

Signs that indicate regulations—no smoking, emergency exit

Signs that provide instructions—how to use the copier, how to search online databases

Instructional signs for equipment or library procedures are among the most difficult kinds of signs to control in a library. When someone is not available to help every user, the tendency of the staff is to put up a handmade sign. Brief instructions for repetitive processes like using a copier can be computer-generated and placed in a sign holder that coordinates with the signs in the rest of the building. The sign can then be mounted on the wall close to the equipment or mounted directly on the equipment.

When designing a sign system, the library staff and local project team should agree on the extent to which signs will be used in the library. The staff should agree during the planning process that most library policies and instructions for complicated procedures should be presented to users by word of mouth or in a handout or flyer, rather than a sign. One of the problem areas in a public library is the circulation desk. Staff have a tendency to place signs on the desk or on a wall behind the desk to provide information about a wide variety of check-out policies and procedures. Most people will not take the time and effort to stop and read a proliferation of signs, and the signs detract from the satisfactory interior design of the area. An attempt should be made during the design process to get the staff to "buy into" the idea of limiting signs to where they are appropriate or necessary.

Signs are fabricated from a variety of materials. (See figure 27.) Plastic is one of the most common materials used for making signs. Some of the types of plastic used are acrylic, polycarbonate, butyrate, fiber-reinforced polyester, and PVC. Acrylic is the most commonly used type of plastic for signs. Plastic signs are durable, relatively inexpensive, easy to fabricate in a variety of forms, and can be supplied in almost any color. Metal signs are produced from aluminum, stainless steel, brass, and bronze. Aluminum is strong, lightweight, durable, and easy to cut. Stainless steel can be used in signs in a manner similar to aluminum. Brass and bronze are most commonly used for making individually cut letters or for cast plaques. Other types of signs available include custom-designed banners, vinyl die-cut letters, transfer lettering, neon, and electronic signs. The application of vinyl die-cut letters or symbols to glass doors, walls, windows, or some type of plastic sign holder is one of the simplest methods for making signs in-house. The signs are inexpensive to produce; however, the letters can be a target for vandalism on signs that are easy to reach from the floor. Many libraries

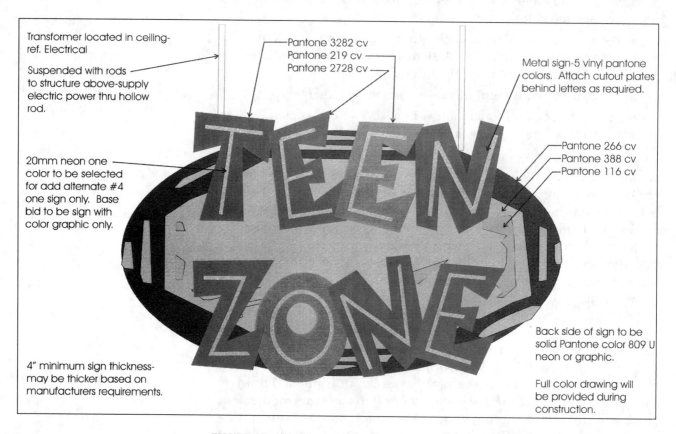

FIGURE 27

Drawing of hanging sign for Grapevine Public Library, Grapevine, Texas.
Sign designed by Phillips Swager Associates, architects. Used by permission of Phillips Swager Associates.

now produce the copy for changeable signs using a computer and a laser printer. The computer-designed signs are then used in a custom or standard plastic or metal sign holder.

Generally, the interior design of a sign system must be coordinated with the other elements in the building. Wayfinding should be considered when developing the architecture of the building; users should not have to depend entirely on signs to move about the library. The arrangement of the library should enhance the ability of users to move easily through it; paths should be as direct as possible from one area to another in order to minimize the need for signs. Architectural and interior design details should be planned to allow for the bracing and wood blocking needed to mount signs in appropriate spaces. Building finishes should also allow for mounting signs where they are needed. Small building details, such as thermostats, fire extinguishers, and light switches should not be located where they will interfere with signage. Power supply for lighted signs and adequate light for viewing signs should be provided.

6 Selecting Materials, Finishes, and Colors

The task of selecting the materials, finishes, and colors to be used in a library's interior should be done by design professionals—architects and interior designers—in consultation with the local planning team and, perhaps, a library consultant. Design professionals should offer the planning team several options for materials and colors and should be prepared to provide other options if their initial selections are rejected. The members of the planning team should, however, acknowledge the expertise of design professionals and carefully consider the recommendations made by architects and interior designers. In most library-planning situations, preconceived ideas about the finishes and colors to be used in the library should not be imposed on design professionals by members of the planning team prior to receiving options proposed by the designers.

In *Interior Design*, John Pile states that the primary functional criterion to consider in selecting materials for a building is their suitability to their basic utilitarian purpose.[1] Secondary considerations include durability, ease of maintenance, resistance to damage and vandalism, safety characteristics, and acoustical performance. The selection of materials also involves the consideration of aesthetic criteria, such as color, textures, patterns, and visual suitability. The cost of a material is often another important consideration in selecting materials.

In small and medium-sized projects, the project budget may be a primary determining factor in selecting materials for the library; some desired materials may be too expensive for the budget. In many library projects, the materials and finishes selected must be ones that can be maintained without expensive equipment, without contracting for expensive outside services, and which can be maintained by the local custodial staff. Custom materials and finishes should be ones that can be easily replicated in the future.[2]

Floor Coverings

Carpet

Because of its appearance and acoustical properties, carpet is used throughout the public areas and in some staff areas of all types of libraries. In many small and medium-sized projects, carpet may be one of the first items that an interior designer selects. The colors in the carpet may provide the basis for the selection of other colors to be used in the interior design of the library. Some interior designers use several different types of carpets in the same library. For example, one carpet may be used as the "field" carpet to cover most floors in the library, while another may be used to make decorative elements such as "paths" or borders. Other designers prefer to use one carpet throughout large areas in order to have as few seams as possible in the carpet.

Denelle Wrightson, an architect and interior designer with Phillips Swager Associates, says she likes to initially present one square sample each of six to eight carpets for a client to consider. The carpets are looked at in several lights. On the basis of the first review, she shows the client larger samples, six to eight squares, of carpets that the local planning team preferred in its first review.

The interior designer or architect should educate the local planning team about their choices in selecting carpet. Maintenance issues are important for every library, and the person who will be in charge of carpet maintenance should be involved in the carpet selection process.

Prior to the 1960s and the introduction of numerous synthetic products, carpets were made of wool fibers. Wool is a natural fiber that is very durable, wears well, and is flame-resistant. Unfortunately, wool carpets are now too expensive for most library projects. According to *The Carpet Primer* (developed by the Carpet and Rug Institute), 99 percent of the face fiber used in carpet now is synthetic.[3] Carpets are made of synthetic fibers using nylon, olefin (polypropylene), acrylic, and polyester.

Nylon carpet is the most frequently used carpet for commercial buildings and is the carpet of choice for many libraries. It is relatively inexpensive and durable, and its fibers are strong and have high stain- and crush-resistance. Nylon carpet can be dyed a wide variety of colors and can be cleaned easily. Acrylic and modacrylic fibers have wool-like characteristics and have less abrasion-resistance than nylon. Like nylon, acrylic fibers can be dyed many colors, have good crush-resistance, and are easy to maintain. Polyester carpet is highly crush- and abrasion-resistant and cleans well. Olefin fibers are used primarily for indoor-outdoor carpet.

Carpets are characterized as woven or tufted. Woven carpets account for a smaller percentage of commercial installations than tufted carpets; however, they are specified for some libraries because they have an extremely dense pile and tightly woven construction. Woven carpets allow an interior designer to specify custom designs and patterns. Wilton, velvet, and axminster are types of woven carpets that are distinguished by the methods of weaving used to produce them. Woven carpets are typically backed during the manufacturing process with polypropylene, polyester, or other synthetic materials. (Note that jute backings are not recommended in situations where flooding could occur; jute is a natural fiber that may rot when it stays wet for an extended period of time.)

Tufted carpet is used in most commercial carpet installations. In the manufacture of tufted carpet, the pile yarn is punched through a backing with rows of needles. When the needle goes through the backing, the yarn is caught and held while the needle makes the next loop. Tufted carpets may be constructed with level loops, with multilevel loops (usually with two or three different loop heights to create pattern effects), with cut pile (loops are cut, leaving individual yarn tufts), or with a combination of cut and loop pile (providing a variety of surface textures, including sculptured effects). In some libraries, level-loop carpet may be used for high-traffic areas, with a coordinating cut-pile carpet used as a border or trim in areas with less traffic.

Tufted carpets usually have a primary backing of woven polypropylene fabric or of nonwoven polypropylene or polyester into which the pile yarn is tufted. A secondary backing of tufted carpets is usually made of latex, polypropylene, or polyester.

Carpets are available in broadloom (long rolls of carpet 6' or 12' wide) and in carpet tiles (18" × 18" or 36" × 36" squares). Carpet tiles are manufactured with fusion bonding that embeds the pile yarn in a backing of liquid vinyl.

Carpeting can be installed by the direct glue-down method, in which the carpet is installed with only an attached cushion that is glued directly to the floor. Carpet tiles are installed using this method. A double glue-down method involves first gluing a cushion to the floor and then gluing the carpet to the cushion. Most public areas of libraries have carpet that is installed using the glue-down method.

Broadloom carpet is also installed using the stretch-in method. The stretch-in method is used where a separate carpet pad is desired under the carpet. A power stretcher is used to stretch the carpet over the pad. The carpet is held in place with some type of tackless strip around the perimeter of the room. According to *The Carpet Primer*, stretch-in installations should be avoided where heavy rolling traffic (like loaded book trucks) is likely.

Library architects and consultants each have their own opinion about whether to use carpet tiles or broadloom in a library. Carpet tiles have been used successfully in many libraries. When carpet tiles are installed properly, they stay in place and can accommodate rolling book trucks. In other libraries, carpet tiles have not stayed in place and have caused problems. Any carpet, regardless of whether it is broadloom or carpet tiles, is only as good as the installation done to put it in place.

It is imperative that library staff notify the general building contractor or the carpet installer if carpet develops problems after a building is open for use. Poor installation or carpet not manufactured to specifications should be reported immediately to those responsible for the building and the carpet.

Design professionals working on a library project should present both options (broadloom and carpet tiles) to the planning team. If the planning team is unsure about the kind of carpet desired, they should visit nearby libraries with carpet squares and with broadloom before making a decision. In some libraries, broadloom carpets (which are less expensive than carpet tiles) are used in areas like bookstack spaces, while carpet tiles are used in high-traffic areas and areas that may change occasionally. Several carpet manufacturers produce both broadloom and carpet tiles in the same colors and patterns.

Carpet selection may involve consideration of a number of other technical aspects of the carpet: dye method, colorfastness, fade-resistance, durability, appearance-retention, crush- and abrasion-resistance, flammability, and acoustical properties.[4] In projects where architects and interior designers familiar with libraries are selecting carpets, the members of the local planning team usually rely on the design professionals to choose carpets that meet the technical requirements of the project.

The library staff of small and medium-sized public libraries are sometimes responsible for selecting carpet for a new building or to replace existing floor coverings. It is important for architects, designers, and library staff who have not worked on commercial projects to understand that residential carpet is not the same as commercial carpet. Residential carpet is often not as expensive as commercial carpets that are manufactured to last for 15 years or more in a high-traffic library.

Library staff responsible for selecting carpet without the assistance of a design professional should do the following:

Work with one or more reliable carpet dealers or manufacturer's representatives who regularly handle commercial carpet. If possible, contact and talk to more than one such dealer or representative. Make sure the vendor understands your project; most libraries require commercial carpet manufactured for extra-heavy traffic areas in public places. Carpet designed for private offices may not be the best choice. Inform the vendor of the maintenance issues in most types of libraries.

Ask the vendor to discuss the technical specifications of the carpet, including, for example, flammability, static control, colorfastness, durability and wearability, stain-resistance, tuft-bind, moisture-absorption rates, the possibility of edges of seams unraveling, ease of maintenance, indoor air-quality issues with the carpet and adhesives, and warranties.

After an initial carpet selection has been made, ask the vendor to provide references to other commercial buildings, preferably libraries, where that same carpet has been used for several years. Call the referenced libraries and ask the library staff about the appearance of the carpet over time and the ease of maintenance of the carpet. If possible, look at the carpet at a library or a similar commercial installation.

The written specifications for a particular carpet provide information that can be used in selecting a satisfactory product. Carpet quality is based on density factors or values that indicate how much yarn is packed into a given area. Carpet selected for busy libraries should have a relatively high density value that provides a more compact carpet. Carpets with high density values provide a firm walking surface and a firm surface for rolling loaded book trucks.

The density factors for tufted carpet include the gauge, the stitches or tufts per square inch, and the pile height and weight. The *gauge* of a carpet indicates the number of ends of surface yarn per inch across the width of the carpet. In selecting carpet for libraries, the gauge should be no less than 1/10, or 10 ends per inch. Stitches per inch (number of tufts lengthwise on the carpet) should be no less than 10 per inch. "Pile height" refers to the height of the carpet from the backing to the top of the yarn. For example, a satisfactory pile height for a library carpet is .187 inch. Pile weight is measured in ounces per square yard. The average pile weight refers to the surface pile of the carpet or its face weight. Pile weights for carpets to be used in busy libraries are often in the range of 20 to 28 ounces per square yard.

The specifications for carpet that will be bid should include performance requirements such as functionality factors (tuft-bind, colorfastness, etc.), appearance and wear properties, indoor air-quality requirements, safety requirements, and aesthetic considerations (pattern, color, texture, etc.).

Except in unusual circumstances (such as earthquake-prone areas where bookstacks are attached to concrete floors), shelving should be moved to allow for carpeting under the stacks, rather than carpeting around the stacks. Carpeting under bookstack areas allows for rearranging the shelving in the future. In some instances where existing carpet is to be replaced by new carpet, a carpet-installation schedule must be coordinated with a schedule for moving furnishings and bookstacks. Often the carpet installation is done by one company and the moving by another.

A specific schedule for carpet installation and moving will depend on the drying time required by the adhesive used to install the carpet. In a simple scenario, however, on day one, movers may move all of the furnishings and shelving from one side of a space or room to the other side. On day two, old carpet is removed and new carpet is installed on the empty side of the room. On day three, all of the furnishings and shelving are moved to the side of the room that now has new carpet. On day four, old carpet is removed and new carpet is installed on the empty side of the room. On day five, all of the furnishings are returned to their designated locations. (A carpeting project provides library staff an opportunity to rearrange the furnishings.)

The color and pattern of a carpet are important considerations that affect how long a carpet continues to look good. A carpet vendor or interior designer may show the planning team books of small carpet samples in order to get an impression of what colors and patterns are acceptable to the team. Larger carpet samples that are considered possibilities for the library space can then be obtained from a vendor or manufacturer. A 4" × 4" carpet sample does not provide a very accurate picture of how a carpet will look in a room. Even an 18" × 18" sample may not be sufficient for evaluating a particular carpet, especially if the product has a large pattern. Vendors will supply photographs of carpet installations that show the pattern and appearance of a carpet when it is installed. Library staff responsible for selecting carpet may want to obtain the names of reliable carpet dealers, representatives, or manufacturers from an architect, designer, or library consultant.

Carpets that are one color throughout will show stains more quickly than carpets that have a patterned or tweedy look or that have individual tufts of many different colors. Light-colored carpets, or carpets with many white tufts among other colors, are more difficult to keep clean than darker carpets. Experienced maintenance staff should be involved in selecting specific carpets and should study the ease of maintenance of products under consideration for purchase.

Hard-Surface Flooring Materials

While large areas of libraries are often carpeted, small areas, such as the entrance foyer, are usually covered with some type of hard-surface flooring material. For example, stone, terrazzo, or tile may be used in a library entrance because of their durability, ease of maintenance, and aesthetic properties. Wood flooring is sometimes used in special libraries and in rooms that house special collections in public or academic libraries. The type of material used in a particular area of a library often depends on the amount of funding available for a project.

Several different types of stone are used as flooring materials in libraries. Stone used as an interior material may have a polished finish with a mirror gloss, a honed finish with a dull sheen, a fine-rubbed finish with no sheen, a rubbed finish with occasional scratches, or a thermal or flame finish that has a coarse finish. Because of the danger of having people slip, polished finishes should not be used on stairs or on areas that might get wet, such as those directly inside a building entrance.

Granite and marble are used in libraries on floors, on walls, and on the tops of service desks and counters. Coatings are available to make a smooth-finished stone slip-resistant. Granite is available in a wide range of colors, including gray, beige, white, pink, red, blue, green, and black. Marble, like granite, is available in a wide variety of colors and patterns, ranging from white to greens and reds with streaked patterns. Marble is an expensive flooring material and requires special care, including buffing and polishing. Marble is not as durable as granite, so its use should be carefully considered.

Limestone is most often used as an exterior material, but travertine (a type of limestone) is used for interior flooring and walls. The patterned surface of travertine is pitted with a network of holes that are sometimes filled with epoxy resin when the stone is used as a flooring material.

Slate is a fine-grained rock that can be split into thin slabs that are used for flooring, as well as roofing, materials. Slate is available in a range of colors that include gray, black, green, brown, and deep red. A slate tile has a rough, uneven texture with a surface level that may vary by about 1/8". Slate may have a sand-rubbed finish or a honed finish that is semi-polished without a sheen.

Another hard-surface flooring material used in libraries and commercial buildings is terrazzo. Terrazzo is a composite or aggregate mixture of small stone particles set in a cement binder that is poured, smoothed out, and polished to create a smooth surface. (See plate 5A.) Because it is durable, water-resistant, and easy to maintain, terrazzo is typically used on floors in high-traffic areas in commercial buildings.

Ceramic and quarry tile are small, flat flooring units made of clay or clay mixtures. Ceramic tiles are durable, water-resistant (if glazed), easy to maintain, and are available in a wide variety of colors, sizes, and patterns. Glazed ceramic tile is often used in public rest rooms and in other locations where water is present. Ceramic tile is waterproof and can be cleaned easily. Quarry tile is sometimes used in library entrance lobbies. The tiles are set in mortar and finished with grouted seams. Slip-resistant quarry tiles with an embossed texture on the surface are available.

Resilient Flooring

"Resilient flooring" is a term used to describe certain materials made from synthetic resins, fibers, plasticizers, and fillers. Thin sheets or tiles are formed under heat and pressure. In libraries, resilient-flooring materials are used in rest rooms, halls, closets, work areas, and in children's activity rooms. Small and medium-sized public libraries with a limited budget may also select resilient-flooring materials for the entrance lobby.

Vinyl floors (available as pure vinyl, vinyl composition, vinyl tiles, and sheet vinyl) are durable, easy to install, and available in a wide variety of colors and patterns. Rubber flooring (made from synthetic rubber) is available with a smooth surface or a patterned, raised surface in either tiles or sheets. This material has great resistance to wear and abrasion; however, only a limited number of colors can be produced.

Wall Coverings

Because paint is relatively inexpensive and can be applied easily, most libraries have painted walls. Paint is also desirable because of the wide range of colors and textures available. Painted areas can be renewed easily and quickly. In busy libraries, an architect or interior designer should be reminded to select paint that can be cleaned and touched up by maintenance staff on a regular basis.

Vinyl wall coverings are more expensive than paint, but they are durable and easy to clean. Vinyl wall coverings are available in a wide variety of colors and patterns and typically come in rolls 52" to 54" wide and 30 yards long. Three grades of vinyl wall coverings are available; type III vinyl wall coverings should be used in busy libraries. These wall coverings may be used throughout a library or may be used in selected areas, such as in halls and around columns that tend to get marred easily.

Vinyl or fabric wall coverings may be used in areas where tackable surfaces are desired. A design professional can select a vinyl with a texture that seems to be self-repairing and that does not show pinholes when displays are removed. In public libraries where 42"-high picture-book shelving is used against a wall, the area of wall above the shelving is often covered with fabric or vinyl to provide a tackable surface. A completely tackable wall is more attractive than a metal-framed bulletin board and looks satisfactory even without a display. (Plastic corner guards should be used on either painted or vinyl-covered surfaces on corners and columns that are apt to be knocked by book trucks.)

Another material that is used for small wall areas in libraries is slat wall, a versatile prefabricated material that consists of slats or strips finished with wood or laminate that are applied horizontally to a backing. The spaces between each of the slats provide a holder for specially designed plastic or wire display items. The slats can be finished to match other laminates or wood finishes in the building. Slat wall is available without inserts between the slats or with plastic or metal inserts. Metal inserts provide the most finished look, but are also the most expensive. Display furnishings made with slat wall are available from library- and bookstore-supply companies. The material can be used on the wall behind a small circulation desk where the staff may want to display a wide variety of information. Slat-wall end panels for bookstacks can be finished with vinyl or solid wood edge bands to provide a more finished appearance. Solid wood edges on the end panels may have a bullnose or other special shape that reflects wood edge bands on other furniture in the library.

Furniture Finishes

The most commonly used finishes for wooden library furniture are catalyzed lacquer and alkyd-urea conversion varnish. Catalyzed lacquer is a nitrocellulose-based finish with a catalyst added to improve its performance. Conversion varnish is a catalyzed alkyd-based finish. Both finishes are considered to be extremely durable and wear-resistant.

Tables with wood-veneer tops are sometimes used in libraries, especially in special collection areas where use is somewhat restricted.

Reading and computer tables in libraries with heavy use, however, often have laminate tops. Laminates are used to provide color to an area of the library and to furnish easy-to-clean surfaces on table-tops, cabinetry, doors, countertops, end panels of bookstacks, and vertical surfaces of service desks.

The major disadvantage of laminate is that it chips easily. In order to prevent laminate edges on furniture from chipping, surfaces should be edged with solid wood, PVC, or other types of bands. A piece of millwork or furniture that is faced with laminate and also has a laminate edge is called self-edged. Self-edged millwork can be used in work areas, but in public areas, self-edged furnishings are likely to chip. When the vertical surfaces of service desks are faced with laminate with no protective band of another material at the bottom, the laminate is likely to be chipped by someone accidentally kicking the desk or by the accidental hit of a book truck.

Color

The selection of colors to be used in a library is one of the most interesting and complex aspects of interior design. Whenever possible, a library should rely on an experienced interior designer whose technical knowledge of light and color can guide a planning team through the selection of colors. If no architect or interior designer is involved in a project, or if a local planning team wants to know more about color, detailed information about selecting colors can be found in *Color in Interior Design* by John Pile.[5]

Sometimes members of a planning team come to a project with a preconceived color scheme in mind. In this situation, the planning team should be encouraged to keep an open mind about options that will be presented by the architect or interior designer. A color scheme that looks great in the director's house may not work in a new library.

The overuse of a particular color scheme in libraries is familiar to anyone who has seen a library designed in the 1960s that still has its original colors. The harvest gold, lime green, and orange upholstered furniture from the '60s provides obvious clues to the age of the library. In the 1970s, library interior design went through a mauve and blue phase.

Like other aspects of interior design, color is affected by the other design elements in a building. A color is affected, for example, by other colors in surrounding areas and by the light that falls on it. Colors viewed under an incandescent light source will appear different from the same colors viewed under a fluorescent light. In selecting colors, therefore, it is important to view them under the same lighting source (artificial or daylight) that will be used in the final building situation.

The psychological effect of colors is usually one of the determining factors in selecting them for a library. Generally, blues, greens, and violets are considered cool, restful colors while red, yellows, and oranges are considered warm, active, stimulating colors. Neutral colors are perceived as having less psychological impact and less emotional content.

As the color of fire and blood, red has the psychological implications of heat and intensity that lead to an association with danger. In library design, bright reds are seldom used as the main color in an area; however, they are sometimes used in children's areas in combination with the other primary colors (yellow and blue), or in adult areas as accent colors.

Yellows are easier to use than reds, because they are considered to have fewer aggressive implications. Like bright reds, yellows are often used in children's areas. Oranges may be used as accents in libraries, but those of us who lived through libraries in the 1960s are reluctant to select bright oranges as the predominant colors in a library.

Unfortunately, some green color schemes are associated with what we refer to as "institutional green" or "military green." Other greens are perceived, however, as calming, stable colors that have associations with colors in nature. According to John Pile, "blue is said to encourage thought, contemplation, and meditation and so [it] is the color of intellectual activity."[6] Perhaps, then, blues are a good choice for quiet study areas in the library.

Texture and pattern on a material may also affect a viewer's perception of color. An item with a smooth finish may appear lighter than an item with a heavy texture. The process of selecting upholstery is similar to the process of selecting carpet. It is impossible to select a patterned fabric from a tiny sample and see how the fabric will really look when it is used in the library. For example, a fabric that has a mauve and blue-gray pattern that can be easily seen up close on a small sample may look slightly purple when viewed on a large chair. It is difficult to successfully select a fabric with a large pattern from a small sample. It is necessary to see a large piece of the material in order to see the complete pattern and to see how the pattern repeats.

When interior designers are charged with selecting colors for a building, the designer usually makes some initial color selections and combinations of colors to show to the local planning team. The task of selecting satisfactory colors is so familiar to experienced designers that they apply their knowledge of color theory easily and quickly. Sometimes a library director and other staff members are given the job of selecting colors for small building projects or for library refurbishing projects. In these situations, the people charged to do the color selection should follow the same procedures as those followed by interior designers and should study some basic information on color theory.

In selecting colors for upholstery and furniture finishes, an interior designer, architect, or local planner must coordinate selections with the other materials and colors that are selected for the building. Colors for furnishings should be selected along with other interior finishes, including the color of laminates or wood to be used on built-in millwork, doors, window and door frames, floors, walls, ceilings, columns, and building trim. Some interior colors will be determined by materials used in the building, for example, granite or marble used on walls and floors or metal used in the rails of a stairway.

Steel shelving is expected to last the lifetime of a library. For this reason, shelving should be purchased in a neutral, rather than a trendy, color that will continue to coordinate with library furnishings as other colors in the library change over time.

In public libraries, one color scheme may be used in the adult area while a different color scheme is used in the children's area. The two color schemes may be coordinated by having the same wood color and finish in both areas.

Colors may be used in a library to identify particular functions. For example, if a building has several service desks, the desks may all be designed using the same colors and finishes in order to provide library users with a visual cue regarding where to obtain information. In multistory libraries, the use of colors in the same relative locations and in the same manner on every floor helps to assist users in finding specific areas.

In some projects, carpet is one of the first interior finishes selected. The predominant colors in a carpet may determine the selection of other colors in the building. In recent years, many libraries have selected carpets with neutral colors. Carpet may initially be viewed in books of samples with each sample about 2" × 2" in size. As previously stated, it is impossible to know how a large expanse of carpet will look based on seeing a tiny sample. A carpet vendor will supply one or several squares of carpet to be viewed in making a selection. When a standard carpet is to be used, the planning team may be able to view the carpet in use at a nearby installation. As with any color selection, carpet samples should be viewed in the same light that will be used in the completed library. Carpet samples should also be considered in relation to other building finishes and materials that have already been selected. Carpet samples should be placed on top of a neutral-colored floor for viewing rather than on top of another carpet.

Most commercial carpet manufacturers will customize colors in a carpet if a minimum number of square yards is to be purchased. For example, if a designer and planning team like the pattern in a particular carpet, but would like more of a certain color, the carpet manufacturer will prepare one or more samples of a standard carpet with customized colors for the team to use in selecting a particular carpet. In large projects, interior designers may work with a manufacturer to develop a totally customized carpet with custom colors.

The process of selecting colors begins with a plan that is based on looking at color samples without having a definite scheme in mind. John Pile suggests that color ideas can begin with solid color areas cut from magazines or brochures, paint charts, or other colored papers. Ideas may come from some element of the community in which the library is located. Daria Pizzetta, an interior designer at Hardy Holzman Pfeiffer, says that her department sometimes looks at textiles to gather inspiration for a color scheme. Small wood samples can be obtained from furniture vendors. Wood finishes and colors can also be based on wood-grain laminate samples. In some academic and special libraries, colors for new interiors may be predetermined by standard colors or finishes adopted by the larger organization of which the library is a part.

In selecting colors for a library, keep in mind that books and other materials housed in the library provide a lot of color. Local staff charged with selecting colors should note that color has an effect on a viewer's perception of objects and spaces. Bright colors make an object look larger, while dark colors make an object look smaller. For example, a small room or space in a library should not be painted a dark color, since that will make the room appear even smaller.

An array of prospective colors is developed by using either color samples collected earlier or by using actual samples of fabric, laminate, wood, etc., provided by vendors. Architects and interior designers often have a library of finishes and colors from which to select samples for projects. It is difficult to see how a color will work in a particular situation without viewing the color in a large piece. Even an 8" × 10" piece of bright yellow laminate may look quite different when the same color is used on a 24" × 66" end panel. If only small samples are shown to a local planning team, the interior designer should be asked to provide larger samples.

Selected color samples should be arranged in a scheme that shows how the colors will look next to each other in a library space. If possible, color samples should be proportionate to the size of the surfaces to be colored in the library. For example, an accent color used in upholstery may be shown in a smaller sample than one of a wall color or a carpet. Interior designers or a local planner can prepare a preliminary color board to be shown to a library board or other approving body.

After all colors and finishes in the building design have been approved, the interior designer will prepare a final color board and a final finish board (and sometimes a board showing furnishings), or one board that shows both colors and finishes. (See plate 4.) In large projects, interior designers may demonstrate selected colors by preparing mock-ups or models or by providing color renderings of building elevations or plan views (bird's-eye views). Computer models of the library spaces may also be used to show the color relationships within a library. In addition to preparing color boards or other demonstrations of colors, an interior designer will prepare a color schedule that lists every color and where it will be used in the library.

NOTES

1. John F. Pile, *Interior Design*, 2nd ed. (New York: Harry N. Abrams, 1995), 218.

2. For more detailed information about building materials and finishes, see William R. Hall, *Contract Interior Finishes: A Handbook of Materials, Products, and Applications* (New York: Whitney Library of Design, 1993).

3. Carpet and Rug Institute, *The Carpet Primer* (Dalton, Ga.: Carpet and Rug Institute, 1995).

4. For detailed information on the technical specifications of carpets and sample specifications for bidding, see S. C. Reznikoff, *Specifications for Commercial Interiors: Professional Liabilities, Regulations, and Performance Criteria*, new rev. ed. (New York: Whitney Library of Design, 1989).

5. John F. Pile, *Color in Interior Design* (New York: McGraw-Hill, 1997).

6. Ibid., 148.

The Interior Design of Spaces for Children and Teens

7 CHAPTER

Children's Areas

Library spaces provide one of the first environments for ensuring that babies will grow up to become lifelong library users. It is essential that a child's early experiences in a library be positive and inviting. The children's area of a public library should be easily accessed from the main entrance to the building. In all but the largest libraries, children should be able to see their area when they walk into the building. The interior design of a children's area should make the location of the space obvious through a welcoming entrance or through the overall design of the space. Ideas for successful children's areas can be obtained by studying how children's museums and other spaces for children are designed. (See plates 5B, 6A, and 6B.)

In planning the location of a children's area in a building, several important adjacencies should be considered. Children should not have to walk through the adult area to get into their space. Nor should young people have to walk through an adult area when they walk to the circulation desk, the children's programming area, or to rest rooms. Many children's areas in libraries of all sizes plan children's rest rooms or family rest rooms adjacent to the children's area. Rest rooms in a children's space should include baby-changing tables that are safe and easy to maintain.

School-age children should not have to walk through the preschool area to get to their books. All children should be able to walk directly from the children's area to the programming area. Most adult library users prefer children's spaces that are separated from the rest of the library by glass walls or by the shape of the building.

Library spaces for babies, toddlers, and school-age children through about fifth grade have received a great deal of attention in the library media. Highly decorated spaces for children are common in medium-sized and large public libraries. Children's areas for preschoolers and young school-age children are often designed with elaborate two- or three-dimensional artwork. The decorative elements in a children's area are often based on a theme. But interior designers should be wary of theme-based decorative elements that may look outdated in a short time. In the book *Creating Ever-Cool: A Marketer's Guide to a Kid's Heart*, Gene Del Vecchio identifies some of the recurring themes that children love, such as animals and historical figures.[1] Small decorative buildings or towns, book characters, and trees are also used by designers in children's areas. In most situations, the complexity of the design of the children's area is determined by the creativity of the architect and the interior designer, and by the amount of funding available for the project. (See figure 28.)

In designing special artwork for children's areas, keep in mind that book and other characters are protected by copyright. It is necessary to obtain permission to use any copyrighted characters and, in some cases, to pay a fee for using the characters in library design.

The interior design of a children's area should take into consideration other factors besides the desire to make a strong aesthetic impact on young library users. Children's areas should be designed to be appropriate for the ages of the users and to be safe for everyone. Children should be comfortable with the furnishings, arrangement, and materials offered. Children need unobstructed spaces that they can explore safely. A children's space should include furnishings and objects that they can use and touch freely without an adult saying "don't do that." In other words, children's space should include items that do not have to be protected from children and that children do not have to be protected from using. Expect that some heavily used items in a children's area—such as stuffed animals and other hands-on items—will need to be replaced on an ongoing basis.

While designers and librarians often build story pits and story platforms, experience has shown that a space that is designed entirely with a flat floor is the best for safety and access. Any construction in a children's area that encourages climbing, jumping, and running (such as ramps or multilevel story areas) must be closely monitored for safety reasons. Changes in the level of the floor create negative situations for children who are frequently corrected by parents, caregivers, or librarians. Flat floors are also a necessity for parents with babies in strollers and people in wheelchairs. If designers or library staff are insistent that a children's area must have platforms or pits for story hours, the area with varying floor levels should be equipped with doors or gates that can be closed when the space is not in use for story hours or other activities. Also, pits or stairs must be accompanied by ramps to make them accessible to everyone.

Children's furnishings should be appropriate for the age and size of the young people using them. Open floor space should be planned in a preschool area for toddlers and preschoolers who often sit on the floor to look at books and play with manipulatives (toys). Chairs with a seat height of 12" to 14" and tables with a height of 21" should be provided for preschoolers. Reading tables in a children's area should be round. Round tables are safe (no corners) for small children and encourage reading and working together.

The color of toys marketed successfully to children provides a clue to colors that may be used successfully in children's areas. Consider using primary colors (red, yellow, and blue) and warm colors, with quiet areas of natural lighting. The use of patterns in

FIGURE 28

Davis Library, Plano, Texas. Architects, Phillips Swager Associates. Used by permission of the photographer. Photo credit: Copyright King Graf 2001.

children's spaces should be studied carefully. For example, if a highly patterned carpet is used, the upholstery on sofas should have very little pattern. The basic interior design of a children's area is sure to be enhanced by a number of "busy" elements added by the library staff, such as hanging objects, stuffed animals, and elaborate displays on tackable surfaces and on the tops of low bookstacks.

Parents and caregivers should have comfortable seating in the children's area, so that they will have a positive library experience with their children and will want to bring them back to the library. Sofas and rocking chairs should be provided for parents and caregivers reading with children. Comfortable seating for adults should also be provided near a children's discovery area, so that parents or caregivers have a place to sit while watching children play with a Lego table, puzzles, or other educational manipulatives. Adults also need a convenient place to sit with toddlers while older children attend programs. Children's spaces in a public library are often areas for parents and caregivers, as well as children, to socialize. (See figures 29 and 30.)

A quiet, semiprivate area should be provided for nursing mothers. For example, a small room with a glass wall and comfortable seating may be located adjacent to an area where young children read and play. The mother has a quiet place with the baby and can still keep an eye on an older child.

Chairs for young children should be all wood for the sake of easy maintenance. Chairs should have sled bases and should be stable enough for a child to push around without the chair tipping over. Children just learning to walk may push a tiny chair (with 12" seat height) around as support.

Young children like small nooks or portals that are in scale with their own size. The interior design of children's space can include two or three small intimate spaces that children crawl into or through. Children's areas should be designed with plenty of display space. Display areas should not be planned with framed bulletin boards. Display areas, such as a wall above 42"-high shelves for picture books, should be provided by installing tackable walls covered with vinyl or fabric. A tackable wall does not draw attention to the area when no display is mounted on the wall.

The shelving for preschool picture books and easy readers should be 42" high. Picture-book shelving is 12" deep. Shelves for picture books are supplied with backs and are slotted to accommodate dividers that help to keep the books upright.

In public libraries, books and other materials for school-age young people should be shelved on bookstacks that are a maximum of 66" high. In some school libraries, library staff prefer a height of 42" or 48" for all bookstacks. Tables for school-age library users can be 25" to 27" high, with chairs having a seat height of 16". In public libraries, the area for young people should also be furnished with one or more round adult-height tables and chairs for parents and caregivers. In some libraries, the adult tables are located close to the parenting section of the collection.

The Interior Design of Spaces for Children and Teens

FIGURE 29

River Falls Public Library, River Falls, Wisconsin. Architects, Brown, Healey,
Stone & Sauer/A Howard Green Company. Used by permission of the architects.
Photo credit: Dale Photographics, Inc.

FIGURE 30

Pella Public Library, Pella, Iowa (a town described as "a touch of Holland in Iowa"). Architects, Brown, Healey, Stone & Sauer/A Howard Green Company. Photo credit: Dale Photographics, Inc.

In some libraries, computers may be used by people of all ages in a children's area. Computer tables for children should be 27" high. More than one seat should be provided at each computer. Young children work with computers collaboratively with parents and caregivers. Moreover, two or three school-age children often use a computer together. Backless stools or chairs can be provided for computer use. The computer area should be supplied with stools or chairs that have 16"-high seats for children and 18"-high seats for adults. Seating for computers should be light enough to allow users to move them around as necessary.

Because families tend to collaborate on computers, a family computer room may be designed. The room would house one or two computers for family use and empty floor space supplied with a few books and toys to occupy toddlers while older children use computers with parents or caregivers.

In small libraries, children's activities and programs are held in the library's meeting room. In larger libraries, programs for small groups of children are held in a special story-time room adjacent to the children's area, while programs for larger groups are held in the library meeting room or auditorium.

In public libraries with ample space, the children's area may include a story-time room, as well as a special activity room for arts and crafts programs. Activity rooms usually have an easy-to-maintain vinyl floor and are furnished with height-adjustable folding tables and stacking chairs. Rooms designed for arts and crafts activities often include a sink and lockable cabinets to hold programming materials. Tackable walls may be provided for displaying items made by young people during library-sponsored events.

Teen Spaces

For many years, libraries have had spaces designated as "young adult" areas. These spaces are relatively small and include several tables with chairs, books and audiovisual materials on shelves and racks, and display capabilities. The target users of young adult spaces vary from library to library.

Until recently, teenagers were, for the most part, left out of library planning. Library staff assumed that teens would use materials, services, and computers in the library's adult area. No attempt was made to create spaces specifically designed for (or by) this age group. Although parents and caregivers recognized that teens want to "hang out"—for example, at the mall—neither design professionals nor library staff addressed the possibility of teens having a large space in a public library dedicated to their use.

In some communities, public libraries are considered important places for young children, and perhaps for adults. Lack of emphasis on the library needs of teens turned some young people away from libraries during this crucial time in their lives. Because of our relative neglect of this segment of youth, public libraries lost an opportunity to make lifelong library users of many teens.

Society's current interest in youth development has renewed the commitment by public libraries to design spaces for teenagers. Teen spaces and services are a special focus of libraries all over the United States. Large teen spaces are part of public libraries in Los Angeles, Phoenix, Tucson, and Brooklyn, for example. The Wallace–Reader's Digest Funds awarded three-year grants of $400,000 each to nine public libraries to create innovative and educationally enriching programs for youth, and the American Library Association recently recognized excellence in after-school programs for young adults.

The process used for designing successful library spaces for teenagers is not the same as the process used for planning other areas of the library. Spaces for teens should be designed *with* teens, not *for* teens. Teen library spaces should be designed to fulfill the concept of the library as "destination" by providing a safe, comfortable place for young people to hang out.

To ensure the success of a teen space, teens should be involved in the planning process from the very beginning of the project. Teens should be empowered to work with library staff and design professionals to plan their own library space; empowerment will lead to a feeling of ownership.

Planning for teen areas may begin with the formation of youth councils that represent young people in the community. In libraries with branches, each branch and the main library may have a youth council. Interior planning for teens may also be carried out using teen focus groups.

The Phoenix Public Library implemented an elaborate, successful process in planning a teen space.[2] The library's goal was to plan a safe, comfortable place for teens that was developed *by* teens. In preparation for designing the space, the planning team visited other libraries and read literature about teenagers.

The participants for teen focus groups were obtained by using newspaper ads, press releases, and flyers and by contacting schools, teen centers, and relevant organizations. Architect Will Bruder, a teen representative, and library staff developed questions for the series of focus groups used in planning the teen space.

Teens participating in the focus groups were given disposable cameras and asked to take pictures of furniture, neon signs, colors, and any other items that they thought were good ideas to be introduced into the planning process. The adults working on the project discovered that teenagers want food, music, and computers.

During part of the planning process, the teens participating in the focus groups were divided into five groups. After the architect explained layout principles, each of the groups used cardboard cutouts of furniture and equipment to develop a possible layout of the teen space. The architect used the focus groups' input to develop plans that were later reviewed by the focus groups.

Teens participating in the Phoenix focus groups voted on the colors provided on color boards. Possible colors for the teen space were also mounted on a web site. Interested teens voted for their favorite colors on postcards that were self-addressed to the library. Teenagers' favorite colors for the library space in Phoenix were blue, bright red, lime green, and burnt orange.

In summary, at the Phoenix Public Library, teens provided input at every planning meeting; voted on the name of the space; picked out colors, fabrics, and furniture; designed the room layout; and picked out the library materials. In addition to books, magazines, audiovisual materials, and comic books, the completed teen space at the Phoenix Public Library houses 20 new computers, a surround-sound stereo system, a color printer for public use, and a large-screen cable television (for watching MTV).

Teen areas may include quiet study areas behind glass walls and round or oval tables for socializing. Study or meeting room space may include white markerboards and tackable vinyl wall coverings. Teens may request computers for individual use or for group use. Other possibilities for teen spaces include special lighting, a dance floor, a living room-type space, a café area, and a variety of seating. The various functions of the spaces will dictate floor coverings. For example, wood will be used on a dance floor, vinyl tile in an eating area, and carpet in a computer and bookstack area. Walls and ceilings may require acoustical treatment. Display capabilities in a teen space may include walls with special surfaces for creative art, tackable walls for display, a message board, and lighted display shelving for books and other materials that are "teen picks." Teen spaces should be flexible, so that the area can be changed easily as "cool" factors for teenagers change over time.

NOTES

1. Gene Del Vecchio, *Creating Ever-Cool: A Marketer's Guide to a Kid's Heart* (Gretna, La.: Pelican, 1997).

2. From the presentation "Teen Central, State-of-the-Art Planning," Phoenix Public Library, developed by Michele Howard, February 20, 2001.

Lighting and Acoustics

Library Lighting

The design of effective lighting for a library is highly technical work done by engineers and architects. In all except the smallest building projects, it is recommended that a lighting consultant, hired by the architect, plan the lighting for a library. The cost of using a lighting consultant should be included in the project budget determined at the project's beginning. The lighting consultant selected should have experience with libraries. In some situations, an architect may work with an electrical engineer with extensive library experience who provides lighting design services.

The cost of hiring a consultant and designing library lighting correctly during initial building planning is less than hiring a consultant later and replacing the initial lighting scheme. Libraries are extremely difficult to light correctly. The need to see clearly the book titles on the top and bottom shelves of a 90"-high bookstack is well known to both library staff and users. If lighting is not designed correctly, dark areas in the stacks, poor lighting at tabletop level, and glare around computers create problems for both users and staff.

The following information is not intended to provide the kind of technical details needed to design lighting for a library. However, the suggestions given here may help a local planning team to work more effectively with lighting professionals. The information here was provided by David Malman, the owner of Architectural Lighting Design, in San Francisco, and has been used with his permission. The material was initially presented at an American Library Association annual conference in 1995 with the title "Lighten Up: How to Write a Library Lighting Program." Malman provided additional information that updated the 1995 material for the writing of this section of the book. Malman was the lighting designer for the San Francisco Main Library as well as other libraries.

In small library building projects where neither a lighting consultant nor an electrical engineer with library experience is involved, the following information should be passed on to the architect designing the new building or renovation.

Recommended lighting levels for various areas of the library, based on the latest edition of the *Illuminating Engineering Society Handbook*, are the easiest variables to measure. The lighting standards of the Illuminating Engineering Society (IES) do not, however, have the legal status of a code. The IES lighting levels do provide a starting point for discussion between a local planning team and the design professionals—architects, interior designers, and engineers—involved in a library project.

Lighting levels are only one of several factors to be considered in guaranteeing successful lighting in a library. Lighting design must also address glare control, spatial definition, orientation, and variety, all of which have more of a bearing on the library user's perception of "good lighting" than do certain lighting levels. (See figure 31.)

In designing lighting, a consultant plans for "maintained" lighting levels, rather than lighting levels on opening day of a library. A lighting consultant calculates "light loss factors" (such as dust on fixtures, age of light bulbs, etc.) to predict the "maintained" lighting level at some point in the library's future.

FIGURE 31

Scott County Public Library, Georgetown, Kentucky. Johnson Romanowitz Architects, Charles L. Witt, principal. Furniture manufactured by the Worden Company. Photo used by permission of the photographer. Photo credit: Copyright Walt Roycraft Photography.

The IES recommends that the lighting levels of reading areas should be 30–40 foot-candles average, measured horizontally at desktop, with task lighting added where it is appropriate in carrels and at tables. For bookstacks, the IES recommends 30 foot-candles average, measured vertically on the stack face at a height of 30". This standard fails to address lighting on the level of the bottom shelf or the evenness of illumination from top to bottom across the entire height of the stack.

The firm Architectural Lighting Design (ALD) suggests an alternate standard to the IES recommendations. ALD suggests that bookstacks should have a lighting level of 36 foot-candles at the top shelf and no less than six foot-candles at the bottom shelf to keep the maximum-to-minimum ratio within reasonable limits. ALD suggests this alternate standard because its experience has indicated that the evenness of illumination across the stack face is more important than achieving a high lighting level at any single point.

The IES recommends, for service desks, a lighting level of 50 foot-candles average, measured at countertop, with careful coordination of computer-screen locations and orientations to avoid reflected glare. Small conference and group study rooms are recommended by the IES to have a lighting level of 30–40 foot-candles average, measured horizontally at desktop. Staff work areas are recommended by the IES to have 50 foot-candles average on desks and worktables, measured horizontally at desktop. According to ALD, the desired lighting level in staff areas can be achieved through a combination of general and task lighting, with 50 foot-candles on desks or tables and approximately 30 foot-candles elsewhere in the work area.

The IES recommends that large meeting rooms have 40 foot-candles average with all lights on, and separately controlled lighting for the podium or presentation area at the front of the room. The meeting-room lights should be dimmable or switchable to produce approximately two foot-candles for note-taking during audiovisual presentations; note-taking light should not spill onto a projection screen. ALD notes that to achieve flexibility in meeting-room lighting, several different "layers" of light or separate lighting systems should allow for combining lights in various ways to suit different activities occurring in the meeting room.

Light fixtures should effectively control glare throughout the library. Lighting in areas with intensive computer use should meet the "preferred" standards for visual display terminal (VDT) lighting in the IES publication "American National Standard Practice for Office Lighting," ANSI/IESNA RP-1-1993. The RP-1 document covers all aspects of office lighting, but its recommendations for VDT lighting generally apply to situations in which people use computers for more than approximately four hours every day. ALD notes that there are many ways to control glare, including deeply shielded parabolic louvers in downlight-type fixtures, various kinds of uplighting, or a combination of techniques. The best controls, according to ALD, meet glare-control requirements and also coordinate with the architectural design of the library.

According to ALD, well-designed fluorescent lighting is the best choice for energy efficiency, good color-rendering, and long lamp-life in bookstack, reading, and staff areas with ceilings lower than 15'. This recommendation should not, however, preclude alternate designs using other light sources in nontypical areas such as large, high-ceilinged places. The effective lighting of high-ceilinged spaces is difficult to design and should be developed carefully by qualified lighting designers.

The most commonly used fluorescent lamps are T8 lamps. T8 lamps with a Color Rendering Index (CRI) minimum of 82 offer the most cost-effective combination of energy efficiency and improved color. T8 lamps are available in warm, medium, and cool color temperatures. The appropriate lamp color for a project should be selected based on studying a mock-up or color board of interior-finish samples lit with each of the three lamp options. ALD suggests that "daylight"-color lamps should be avoided, because they are expensive and inefficient.

T5 high-output lamps are also used now. T5 lamps produce more light than T8 lamps, but they are more expensive than T8 lamps and produce more glare. T5 lamps should be used only in indirect uplight fixtures.

All fluorescent lamps require ballasts to start the lamps and regulate current while the lamps are running. Electronic ballasts from major manufacturers have a proven track record of reliability, flicker-free quiet operation, and significant energy savings. Because many different types of electronic ballasts are available, lighting designers should select the best balance between light output and energy consumption.

Because of its low efficiency and short lamp-life, in general, incandescent lighting should be avoided, except in special situations. Incandescent sources should be used only where no other source can meet the needs for precise beam control, small fixture size, easy dimming, or historical accuracy. (See plate 7.)

Daylighting can substantially reduce energy costs when it is combined with an appropriate control system for electric lights. Although ultraviolet light is the most damaging wavelength of light, any light can cause cloth, paper, and ink to degrade over time. Except in rare-book collections, it is better to keep books away from direct sunlight than to install costly ultraviolet filtering in electric lights.

The lighting fixtures selected for a library must last a long time; therefore, it is important that high-quality fixtures be specified. Table or desk lamps should be of durable construction and should be designed to spread light evenly across the worksurface. In public areas, table lamps should be securely mounted to furniture and should not obstruct the librarian's view across the room. Emergency and exit lighting should meet local requirements. Exit signs should use low-energy fluorescent, LED, or electroluminescent sources.

Library lighting should be in compliance with all applicable accessibility guidelines, including the 1990 Americans with

Disabilities Act. Compliance with the ADA requires that in walks, corridors, passageways, and aisles, no portion of a wall-mounted light at a height between 27" and 80" above finished floor should project more than 4" from the wall. In elevators, the minimum light level on the floor and on the controls should be five foot-candles. Signs should be adequately lit. Lighting controls should be mounted no more than 48" above the finished floor.

In large libraries, lighting circuits should be turned on and off by a lighting-control system that allows flexible, timed programming for each circuit. A master control station should be located at the circulation desk or other central location, for manual override of groups of lights. This type of lighting-control system is sometimes part of an overall "building energy-management system" that controls lighting and heating, ventilation, and air-conditioning (HVAC) loads. Lights near windows or skylights should be switched separately from other lights. Consider dimmable fluorescents for areas that receive significant daylight. Occupancy sensors should be considered to reduce energy consumption in areas that are not in continuous use, such as closed stacks or meeting rooms.

Maintenance issues should be a prime consideration in designing a lighting system for a library. The number of different lamps selected should be minimized to simplify lamp-stocking. Also, consideration should be given during the design process to the purchase of any special equipment that may be needed to change out lamps in fixtures that are difficult to reach using more than a ladder.

Sound Control

Libraries are no longer quiet spaces where the staff shush noisy undergraduates or children. Although quiet areas in libraries remain, library users and staff now talk out loud to each other on a regular basis in the public areas of all types of libraries. Computers and printers add to the noise level of a library; children are allowed to act like young people in their designated area; and in areas where the collaborative use of computers is encouraged, conversations occur.

Acoustical issues for libraries were discussed by Jack Wrightson (principal acoustical consultant with Wrightson, Johnson, Haddon, and Williams, Inc.) and Jeffrey Scherer (principal with Meyer, Scherer & Rockcastle) at a 1998 American Library Association program entitled "Not Just Shhh Anymore: Improving Library Acoustics." Wrightson identified three categories of acoustical problems that may occur in libraries: intrusive noise or noise that is not wanted in a particular space (such as noise from adjacent meeting or activity rooms), overly reverberant spaces (such as spaces with vaulted ceilings), and lack of speech privacy, especially in staff areas.

Intrusive noise in a building may be controlled by the grouping of spaces and by the layout of rooms within the library. Architects have traditionally grouped noisy elements of a building next to other noisy spaces. For example, main HVAC units are usually placed close to a receiving or mechanical area, rather than next to a quiet reading area for the public. Sometimes large bookstack areas where little conversation occurs serve as a buffer between a noisy area such as the reference center and a quiet area like the periodical reading area.

Where lifelong use of libraries is the accepted norm, public library users accept the fact that children's areas will be noisy. Babies and toddlers (and their parents) cannot enjoy a trip to the library if children are constantly told to sit still and be quiet. In order to keep the noise of a children's area from annoying adults, children's areas are usually placed in a different wing of a library from adults, placed on a different floor of multistory libraries, or separated from adult areas by glass or walls.

Overly reverberant spaces may be avoided by consideration of acoustical treatments in building design. The materials used on walls, floors, and ceilings; the location of doors and windows; and the acoustical treatment of ductwork all affect sound control in a library. Hard, reflective surfaces on walls, floors, and ceilings result in a noisy space. A monumental library entrance or circulation desk area constructed with granite walls and floors and plenty of glass may be an aesthetic masterpiece but an acoustical nightmare. Architects and interior designers are responsible for selecting building materials and architectural elements that will provide adequate sound control in a library. Local planners should be aware of the need for sound control in their buildings and should ask architects about acoustics during building design.

Public, school, and academic libraries are expected to provide areas for quiet study and reading, as well as for computer use. Jeffrey Scherer suggests that libraries should be designed with computer-free zones, where users wanting traditionally quiet library spaces can enjoy relative quiet in a library. With computers in use in many areas, library planning should include the design of quiet rooms with soft, comfortable seating, as well as seating at carrels and tables. For the sake of visual control, quiet rooms may have some glass walls to allow for visibility into the room.

In large library projects, an acoustical consultant should be hired to plan the sound-control elements of a new or renovated building. In libraries with large meeting rooms or auditoriums, an acoustical consultant is a necessity. In many small and medium-sized projects, the architect and the interior designer are responsible for handling the acoustical decisions in the project. Local planners should be aware of the need for sound control in their buildings and should ask their architects and interior designers about the acoustical treatments to be used in their library.

CHAPTER 9

Conclusion

The interior designers who were interviewed in the course of gathering information for this book were asked how library interior design differs from the design of other types of buildings. One designer replied, "It's not your house." The scale is entirely different in a library than in smaller buildings. Another designer said that library projects are difficult because there are so many parts and pieces of different sizes and uses that have to fit into a library. Academic libraries are sometimes difficult to design because of the large number of organization officials involved in the process.

All of the interior designers who were interviewed asked that clients trust the judgment of the architect and the interior designer. Everyone involved in the planning process should come to the project with an open mind. When a client offers a suggestion to a designer, the client should explain the logic behind an idea and explain where the idea came from. Clients should work along with the pace of the architects and interior designers. Many decisions must be made during the design process, but there is an order to the timing of decision making. Some decisions are made early in the process and others are made later.

Interior designers, architects, and building owners need to have a shared understanding about their expectations for a new facility. Architects and interior designers need to know the internal chain of command of the client—who is going to make the final decisions. Likewise, the clients should know the chain of command of the design team. In order to keep the project on schedule, the client, as well as the designers, needs to make timely decisions. Both the client and the design professionals should feel free throughout the project to ask why something is being done, why a particular finish has been selected, etc.

Except in unusual circumstances, funding for a new project is always a concern. Both the design professionals and the client must understand the budget expectations at the beginning of a project. Jeffrey Scherer, principal with Meyer, Scherer & Rockcastle, tells clients that in cases where funding is an issue, they can dictate two out of three considerations in building a new facility: cost, size, and quality. For example, a client may pay for the high cost of quality and sacrifice some of the size of the building. Or a client may want a larger building, but is willing to sacrifice some of the quality in materials in order to get the desired number of square feet in the facility.

Much of the information provided in this book is related to the functional aspects of library interior design. Effective adjacencies, the use of durable materials, and satisfactory lighting should result in a functional building; however, the truly distinctive elements of outstanding interior design in any library are the result of the creative work of architects and interior designers. (See plate 8.) Unusual architectural features; effective use of windows and varied ceiling heights; creative use of color, materials, and decorative details; and custom furnishings and floor coverings are just some of the elements that design professionals combine with functional components to create an award-winning library interior.

Interview Questions for Obtaining Information from Library Staff

The following list of questions can be used by architects, interior designers, and consultants when they are gathering information in preparation for programming, planning, and selecting furniture for a library. Interviews and meetings with staff in the early stages of a project are an essential part of the planning process. Participants in information gathering are more likely to take ownership in a project when they have had an opportunity to offer their input. Library staff who have toured or worked in other libraries may have an informed opinion about what they want in their new library. On the other hand, staff who are familiar only with their existing work situation may not be able to provide very meaningful information. Some libraries are so inadequate that the employees don't have a clue about what they want and need in a new space. If staff have no informed opinion concerning the new space, it is up to the architect, designer, or consultant to offer options to which the staff can react during the interview process. At some point in the planning process, it may become necessary to remind participants that the furnishings selected now will be used by many other employees in the future. (This list of interview questions was developed in response to discussions with Bev Moris of Simon, Martin-Vegue, Winkelstein, Moris.)

Shelving

What kind of steel shelving is preferred—welded-frame or European-style starter/adder (like that of BCI)?

What type of shelves is desired for books—flat shelves or shelves with an integral back? (If sliding book supports are to be used, shelves must have an integral back.)

What height of shelving will be used for various books—42" and 66" for children's areas? What about other areas—66", 78", 84", or 90" standards, or special heights like 48"?

What depth of shelves will be used—12" deep for picture books and reference books? What about adult fiction and nonfiction—10" deep or 12" deep?

Which shelving should have matching steel canopy tops, which should have no tops, and which shelves should have custom wood or laminate tops?

What kind of book supports will be used?

Will all ranges of shelving have end panels? Will the panels be steel, wood, laminate, or custom-designed?

How will signage be handled on the end panels? Ready-made signs or custom signs?

What special shelving will be needed? How will each type of audiovisual material be housed (videos, single audiotapes, audio books, CDs, DVDs, CD-ROMs, books on CD)? Will any lighted shelving be needed to highlight special collections?

How will paperbacks be housed? Paperback shelving on steel frames, paperback rounders, slat-wall shelving?

How will periodicals be shelved? Hinged or fixed periodical shelves? Plexiglas covers for current issues of newspapers? Oblique files for back issues of newspapers?

Will some special collections be shelved on wood shelves? (Consider preservation issues in this regard.)

Circulation Desks

Will the circulation desk consist of one monumental desk where all circulation functions take place? Or will the library have separate check-out and return desks?

What is the maximum number of computer stations needed at the desk? What equipment is expected to be used—flat-screen computers or larger personal computers? Will other equipment, such as a typewriter, be used at the desk? How will all of the computer peripherals be accommodated on the desk? How will printing be handled? How will the desk accommodate any equipment needed for the book-theft detection system?

In a public library, where will books held on reserve be stored in relation to the desk? Are the reserved books centrally located so that all people working at the desk can retrieve them?

Will any reference materials in book format be stored at the circulation desk?

What small paper items will be stored at the desk next to each check-out or return station? Registration forms for library cards, library cards, informational brochures about library policies, etc.? What size are these items? Will they be stored in custom-designed slots in the desk or in drawers?

Where will money be handled? Will the desk have one or more cash registers? Does only one person at a time handle money? Or does the cash drawer or register need to be located so that more than one person on duty can handle cash?

Are staff on duty expected to stand at all times, or are knee spaces provided at each computer station in order to allow an employee to sit on a high swivel stool?

Where will the ADA/children's check-out module be placed in the desk? Will the unit allow for pulling a wheelchair under the desk, or will it allow only for pulling alongside?

Does the library need special storage areas at the circulation desk?

What is the relationship between the circulation desk and the work area?

How will power and data be distributed from the building through the desk? How will wire management be handled?

Is a work area required behind the circulation desk that will need a secondary work desk?

Are returned books collected on book trucks behind the desk as they are returned? How many book trucks should the area accommodate? Will most books be checked in at the desk, or will they be moved to the workroom to be checked in?

Will the desk have returned-materials slots? Will books drop from the desk into the work area?

Will furniture for self-check machines be needed now or in the future? Where should these machines be located?

Reference Desks

Most of the questions about circulation desks listed above are also relevant to designing reference desks.

Will reference staff be at a seated-height desk of 29", or will the staff be seated on high swivel stools behind a 39" desk? Will a desk with a work area at 29" have a transaction top at, say, 36" high?

Will a private, sit-down station for lengthy reference interviews be required?

What will be stored at the desk? Ready-reference materials, interlibrary loan forms, fax request forms, etc.?

How many computers will be at the desk? How will printing be handled? Will the desk hold a fax machine? A scanner?

Public Computer Stations

What kind of work will users be doing at the computers? Will some computers be used mainly for quick catalog searches? Should these be at standing height? Which computers will be used for researching topics on the Internet and electronic databases?

Who will be using the computers? Adults or children? Will all information be loaded on the LAN or will some computers for children have individual pieces of software loaded on each CPU?

How many people may use the computer at one time?

What type of seating will be used at each computer?

What equipment will be used at each workstation—monitor and keyboard, CPU, printer, speakers, scanners? Will printing be networked? Where will the printer sit? How much space will this equipment occupy on opening day?

What should the dimensions of each workstation be?

How will power and data be handled at each workstation? Wired data to the workstation? Wireless data transmission? How many outlets will be needed at each workstation? Integrated electrical system in the furniture, or individual plugs in the floor for each computer? How will wire management be handled?

Reading Tables

Decisions about reading tables are more aesthetic than functional. Ask whether the client wants leg-based or panel-end tables or some of both. Adults like rectangular tables in order to maintain their personal space. Teens and children like round tables (which are also safer for little kids) because they encourage conversation and collaboration. Ask about access to power and data and task-lighting at reading tables.

Reading Chairs

Does the owner want upholstered or unupholstered reading chairs? Arms or no arms?

In the children's department, what size chairs are needed?

Lounge chairs—emphasize the need for wood or wood-capped arms.

Teen and Children's Areas (Public and School Libraries)

What age youth will be served by the children's area? What age youth will be served by the teen or young adult area?

Repeat the questions asked about reference desks as they relate to youth areas.

How many computers will be housed in the children's area? The teen area? Repeat the relevant questions regarding computer workstations as they relate to youth areas.

Will the library have a separate story-time room and a separate activity room (with resilient flooring)? How many children should the story-time room accommodate? Will the children sit on the floor or on small stacking chairs? Should some adult-height chairs be supplied for the room? How many children should be accommodated at tables for craft activities in the story-time room or in a separate activity room?

Should a special waiting area with lounge chairs be supplied for parents or caregivers waiting for children attending programs?

In addition to seating at tables, should the children's area include lounge chairs, rocking chairs, or sofas for children and parents reading together?

Should the furniture in the children's area reflect the furnishings in the adult area? Or should the children's area be designed as a separate entity?

Should the children's area include some specially designed features or artistic features based on a theme?

Work Areas

What is the library's philosophy regarding management? How much administration is done by teams? How does management by teams affect the selection of furnishings?

If the owner selects office-panel systems for staff workstations, does the library have maintenance staff that can reconfigure panels easily? Will the building power and data grid support reconfiguring workstations easily?

Would ordinary desks or a system that looks like a panel system, but is really freestanding (like Steelcase Context), work better than a true office-panel system in some situations?

Circulation Work Areas

Where will materials be returned? From an outside book or audiovisual drop? From a materials drop in the foyer? From the circulation desk?

What is the relationship between the materials-return points and the check-in stations? Where will returned materials be checked in? What equipment is needed for check-in? How many check-in stations are needed? Where will checked-in materials be moved for sorting?

How many sorting shelves will be needed? How much room will be needed for parking book trucks by check-in stations and by sorting shelves?

How many individual desks or workstations will be needed in the circulation workroom? Are work spaces needed for volunteers? Can some work areas be shared space at built-in counters? Will more than one manager require a separate office? What furnishings are needed in the office? Where will employees lock up their belongings and hang up their coats? Will an individual coffee bar be located in the department? Where is the nearest staff rest room?

Will a conference room be needed? How large should the room be? Or should conferences take place at a table in the workroom?

Where will audiovisual checking take place? In another department?

What is the relationship between the circulation workroom and the delivery area where books and audiovisual materials will be returning from branches?

Reference and Collection-Development Work Areas

How many separate work desks or stations are needed here? What should each workstation include—files, shelves, desktop, guest chairs, etc.?

Is a separate office for one or more managers needed? What should each office include in regard to furnishings?

How many shelves will be needed for incoming reference books, special collections, and collection-development tools?

A related question: does the library continue to have a collection of back issues of magazines and newspapers? Where are these stored? Are they available directly to the public or are they retrieved by staff? Where are these back issues in relation to the reference desks? How much shelving will be needed for this collection? Is the library reducing the size of the collection as more titles become available in electronic format?

Where will employees lock up their belongings and hang up their coats? Will an individual coffee bar be located in the department? Where is the nearest staff rest room?

Will a conference room be needed? How large should the room be? Or should conferences take place at a table in the workroom?

Are there any other special requirements for the reference work area?

Technical-Services Work Areas

How will new materials flow through the work area? What are the relationships between acquisitions, receipt and check-in, cataloging, and processing? Where is the library loading dock and receiving area in relation to the technical-services work area?

Individuals in each part of the department need to be asked about the specific requirements for their work area: types of equipment used, types of materials stored, number of book trucks stored near their work area, height of work area needed, special storage needs. How many desks or workstations are needed? Will space be needed for volunteers?

Where will employees lock up their belongings and hang up their coats? Will an individual coffee bar be located in the department? Where is the nearest staff rest room?

Will a conference room be needed? How large should the room be? Or should conferences take place at a table in the workroom?

Is more than one separate office for the department needed? How much privacy does each individual need? (Sometimes catalogers like a private area and individuals who process books like to chat while they work.)

Technology Work Areas

What is the relationship between technology work areas and the location of the main computer/server room?

How many and what configuration of LAN-management furnishings will be needed in the computer room?

How many separate offices and individual desks or workstations will be needed? How much privacy will each person need? What are the power and data requirements for the area?

Where will computers awaiting repair (or computers kept for spare parts) be stored? Where will new computers awaiting installation be stored?

Will large workbenches, as well as individual desks, be needed for loading software and making repairs on hardware? What types of materials will require storage close to workbenches?

Where will employees lock up their belongings and hang up their coats? Will an individual coffee bar be located in the department? Where is the nearest staff rest room?

Will a conference room be needed? How large should the room be? Or should conferences take place at a table in the workroom?

What is the relationship between the technology work area and the loading dock and receiving area?

Work Areas for Youth Services Staff
(Public and School Libraries)

How many individual desks and offices will be needed?

What are the special storage requirements for the area? Is storage needed for large pieces of paper and other programming supplies? Storage for theme boxes for programs? What size are the theme boxes? How many boxes will require storage? Storage needed for puppets? How many puppets? Audiovisual equipment to be stored? Vertical storage for large props? Storage for costumes? Storage for a portable puppet theater?

What types of furnishings are needed for preparing for children's programs? Standing-height counters? Large tabletops?

Where will employees lock up their belongings and hang up their coats? Will an individual coffee bar be located in the department? Where is the nearest staff rest room?

Will a conference room be needed? How large should the room be? Or should conferences take place at a table in the workroom?

Computer-Training Rooms

What type of computer stations will be used? Monitors set on the tabletop, partially recessed monitors, or fully recessed monitors?

Will computers be on long tables or individual stations? Will rooms be arranged in classroom style or with computers around the perimeter of the room (in which case millwork counters can be used)?

What type of chairs will be used? Task chairs? Stacking chairs?

What other equipment will have to be accommodated by the furnishings? Printers? Presentation stand? Ceiling-mounted video projector? Screens?

Will the training room be adjacent to breakout rooms? Will breakout rooms have small tables that can be rearranged or one large conference table?

Outreach Areas (Public Libraries)

What is the relationship of the outreach area to the loading dock?

What furnishings will be needed for staging? Large tables? Numerous book trucks?

How much shelving will be needed for outreach collections? What types of materials are in the collections?

How many private offices and workstations will be needed? What are the requirements for these spaces?

Will storage be needed for boxes or bags of programming materials to be taken to outreach sites? What size? How many? Can millwork cubbyholes be used for these materials? Or industrial steel shelving?

Also, talk about the specifics of built-in millwork: heights, sizes, how spaces will be used, etc.

Directory of Contributors

APW-Wright Line
160 Gold Star Boulevard
Worcester, MA 01606
508-852-4300

Architectural Lighting Design
370 Brannan Street
San Francisco, CA 94107
415-495-4085

ASI Sign Systems, Inc.
3890 W. Northwest Highway
Suite 102
Dallas, TX 75220
214-352-9140

Brown, Healey, Stone & Sauer
A Howard Green Company
8710 Earhart Lane SW
Cedar Rapids, IA 52404
319-841-4000

F & S Partners
8350 North Central Expressway
Suite 500
Dallas, TX 75206
214-559-4851

Fetzers' Inc.
1436 South West Temple Street
Salt Lake City, UT 84115
801-484-6103

Hardy Holzman Pfeiffer Associates, LLP
902 Broadway, 19th Floor
New York, NY 10010
212-677-6030

Hermes Architects
7915 Westglen Drive
Houston, TX 77063
713-785-3644

Johnson Romanowitz Architects
300 East Main Street
Lexington, KY 40507
859-252-6781

Kirksey
6909 Portwest Drive
Houston, TX 77024
713-850-9600

Libra-Tech Corporation
1115 Thornridge Court
Argyle, TX 76226
940-464-3033

Meyer, Scherer & Rockcastle, Ltd.
119 North 2nd Street
Minneapolis, MN 55401
612-375-0336

MJ Industries
P. O. Box 259
Carleton Drive
Georgetown, MA
978-352-6190

Parkhill, Smith & Cooper, Inc.
4222 85th Street
Lubbock, TX 79423
806-473-2200

Phillips Swager Associates
7557 Rambler Road
Suite 670
Dallas, TX 75231
469-232-5200

Ray Bailey Architects
4100 South Shepherd
Suite 100
Houston, TX 77098
713-524-2155

Simon, Martin-Vegue,
Winkelstein, Moris
989 Market Street, Third Floor
San Francisco, CA 94121
415-546-0400

Thos. Moser Cabinetmakers
72 Wright's Landing
P. O. Box 1237
Auburn, ME 04211
207-784-3332

The Worden Company
119 East 17th Street
Holland, MI 49423
616-392-1848

Wrightson, Johnson, Haddon
& Williams, Inc.
4801 Spring Valley Road
Suite 113
Dallas, TX 75244
972-934-3700

BIBLIOGRAPHY

Ballast, David K. *Interior Design Reference Manual.* Belmont, Calif.: Professional Publications, 1992.

Bazillion, Richard J., and Connie L. Braun. *Academic Libraries as High-Tech Gateways: A Guide to Design and Space Decisions.* 2nd ed. Chicago: American Library Association, 2001.

Brawner, Lee B., and Donald K. Beck Jr. *Determining Your Public Library's Future Size: A Needs Assessment and Planning Model.* Chicago: American Library Association, 1996.

Brown, Carol R. *Planning Library Interiors: The Selection of Furnishings for the Twenty-First Century.* Phoenix: Oryx, 1995.

Carpet and Rug Institute. *The Carpet Primer.* Dalton, Ga.: Carpet and Rug Institute, 1995.

Cohen, Aaron, and Elaine Cohen. *Designing and Space Planning for Libraries: A Behavioral Guide.* New York: R. R. Bowker, 1979.

Del Vecchio, Gene. *Creating Ever-Cool: A Marketer's Guide to a Kid's Heart.* Gretna, La.: Pelican, 1997.

Eckelman, Carl A. "Library Chairs: An Overview of the Library Technology Reports Test Method with Test Reports on 30 Chairs." *Library Technology Reports* (March–April 1995).

Feinberg, Sandra, Joan F. Kuchner, and Sari Feldman. *Learning Environments for Young Children: Rethinking Library Spaces and Services.* Chicago: American Library Association, 1998.

Hall, William R. *Contract Interior Finishes: A Handbook of Materials, Products, and Applications.* New York: Whitney Library of Design, 1993.

Holt, Raymond, and Anders C. Dahlgren. *Wisconsin Library Building Project Handbook.* 2nd ed. Madison: Department of Public Instruction, 1989.

Howard, Michele. "Teen Central, State-of-the-Art Planning." Presentation at the Phoenix Public Library, February 20, 2001.

Leighton, Philip D., and David C. Weber. *Planning Academic and Research Library Buildings.* 3rd ed. Chicago: American Library Association, 1999.

Lushington, Nolan, and Willis N. Mills. *Libraries Designed for Users: A Planning Handbook.* Hamden, Conn.: Library Professional Publications, 1980.

Malman, David. "Lighten Up: How to Write a Library Lighting Program." Paper presented at the annual conference of the American Library Association, 1995.

Massman, Ann. "The Wood Shelving Dilemma." *Library Resources and Technical Services* 44, no. 4 (October 2000): 209–13.

McCabe, Gerard B. *Planning for a New Generation of Public Library Buildings.* Westport, Conn.: Greenwood, 2000.

Pile, John F. *Color in Interior Design.* New York: McGraw-Hill, 1997.

———. *Interior Design.* 2nd ed. New York: Harry N. Abrams, 1995.

Reznikoff, S. C. *Specifications for Commercial Interiors: Professional Liabilities, Regulations, and Performance Criteria.* New rev. ed. New York: Whitney Library of Design, 1989.

Sannwald, William W. *Checklist of Building Design Considerations.* 4th ed. Chicago: American Library Association, 2001.

Scherer, Jeffrey, and Jack Wrightson. "Not Just Shhh Anymore: Improving Library Acoustics." Paper presented at the annual conference of the American Library Association, 1998.

INDEX

as design elements, 70–77
do-it-yourself design and, 42
furniture finishes for, 103–4
interview questions for staff
regarding, 130
lighting and, 121
Technical-services departments
freight elevator location and, 4
interview questions for staff
regarding, 132–33
planning process and, 17–18
staff work areas and, 79, 82–83
Technology. *See also* Computers
internal flexibility and, 8
interview questions for staff
regarding, 133
staff work areas and, 79, 84
Teen spaces, 115–17, 130–31
Teleconferencing, 31
Telephones. *See* Power/data transmission locations
Terrazzo. *See* Floor coverings
Terrebonne Parish, Houma,
Louisiana, Plate 4, 88
Texas Tech University, Lubbock,
Texas, 6, 30, 66
Theft. *See* Security
Tile. *See* Floor coverings
Training. *See* Education

U
Under-floor duct systems, 26–27

V
Varnish, 103
Vertical files' signs, 91
Vinyl. *See* Wall coverings
Volunteers' area, 41

W
Wall coverings, 102–3
Wallace–Reader's Digest Funds
youth grants, 116
Water as aesthetic element, 27
Wayfinding. *See* Signage
Weeding, 9
Wheelchair accessibility. *See*
Americans with Disabilities
Act (ADA)
White, Howard S., 74
Wide area networks (WANs), 84
Windows
administrative work areas and,
86
location of, 25
sound control and, 123
tables/carrels and, 2–3
unusual, 125

"Wood Shelving Dilemma, The," 56
Woodwork, 77–78. *See also*
Furniture; Shelving
Work areas. *See also specific area,
i.e.,* Reference
interview questions for staff
regarding, 131–34
planning process and, 78–79
Workflow
furniture/shelving layout and,
4–5
planning process and, 12
technical-services departments
and, 18
Workstations. *See also* Computers
computer furniture and, 64–70
interview questions for staff
regarding, 129–31
power/data transmission locations and, 25–27
Wrightson, Denelle, 97
Wrightson, Jack, 122

Y
Young adult area
location of, 36
teen spaces, 115–17

Carol R. Brown is currently assistant director of the Fort Bend County Libraries in Richmond, Texas. She holds a B.A. in fine arts and English from Cornell College in Iowa and an M.A. in library science from Indiana University. She previously held library positions at Indiana University and the Houston Public Library. For 10 years she worked as a library planning consultant with her own firm, Carol Brown Associates. Brown is the author of two other books on library interior design and furnishings.